CN01260956

WHY SHOULD I GO TO LONDON

WHY SHOULD I GO TO ↴
LONDON

THE CITY YOU DEFINITELY
NEED TO VISIT
BEFORE YOU TURN 30

(m)

FOR BLACK BOYS...
BY
RYAN CALAIS CAMERON
COME IN
319
Ebury Place

THIS IS WHY!

London is one of the most cosmopolitan and culturally diverse cities in the world. Full of life, history and art, buzzing with creative energy. More than three hundred languages are spoken within the British capital, and those heritages are reflected in its lively street-food scene. You can take a culinary trip around the world at any time.

As we all know, London is not the cheapest destination in the world. However, exploring this exciting city does not have to cost a fortune. Walk, cycle, and use public transport, rather than taking expensive taxis. Book affordable accommodation, join free walking tours, and visit world-class museums and galleries for free. Take advantage of the many parks and immerse yourself in the vibrant markets and street art scene; the city offers a myriad of experiences for every taste and budget.

London changes its face and pace, not only with the seasons, but around every street corner too. It's both achingly hip and steeped in tradition, gloomy grey can suddenly make way for an abundance of green. It might be hard to grasp the city's essence. Just keep on walking, take in the scenery, soak up the atmosphere: keep calm and carry on! One thing is certain: you will want to come back for more.

CONTENTS

BOROUGHS 8
PRACTICAL INFO 12

WHEN TO TRAVEL 28
LONDON LIFE 38

FOOD AND DRINKS 100
GOING OUT 124

SHOPPING 134

GREEN LONDON 166
OUTSIDE OF LONDON 184

Index 188
Who made this book? 191-192

BOROUGHS

Inner London consists of the City of London and twelve boroughs, or local authority districts. They are indicated with postcodes. Central London is divided into EC (East Central) and WC (West Central). Around those two, you'll find N (North), E (East), SE (South East), SW (South West), W (West) and NW (North West). The higher the number that follows the first letter(s), the further out it is. These are the boroughs with their main postcode.

The City of London (EC1)

Also known as *the square mile*, it is the historical and financial heart of London. Home to the Bank of England and the London Stock Exchange, but also to St. Paul's Cathedral and the Tower of London.

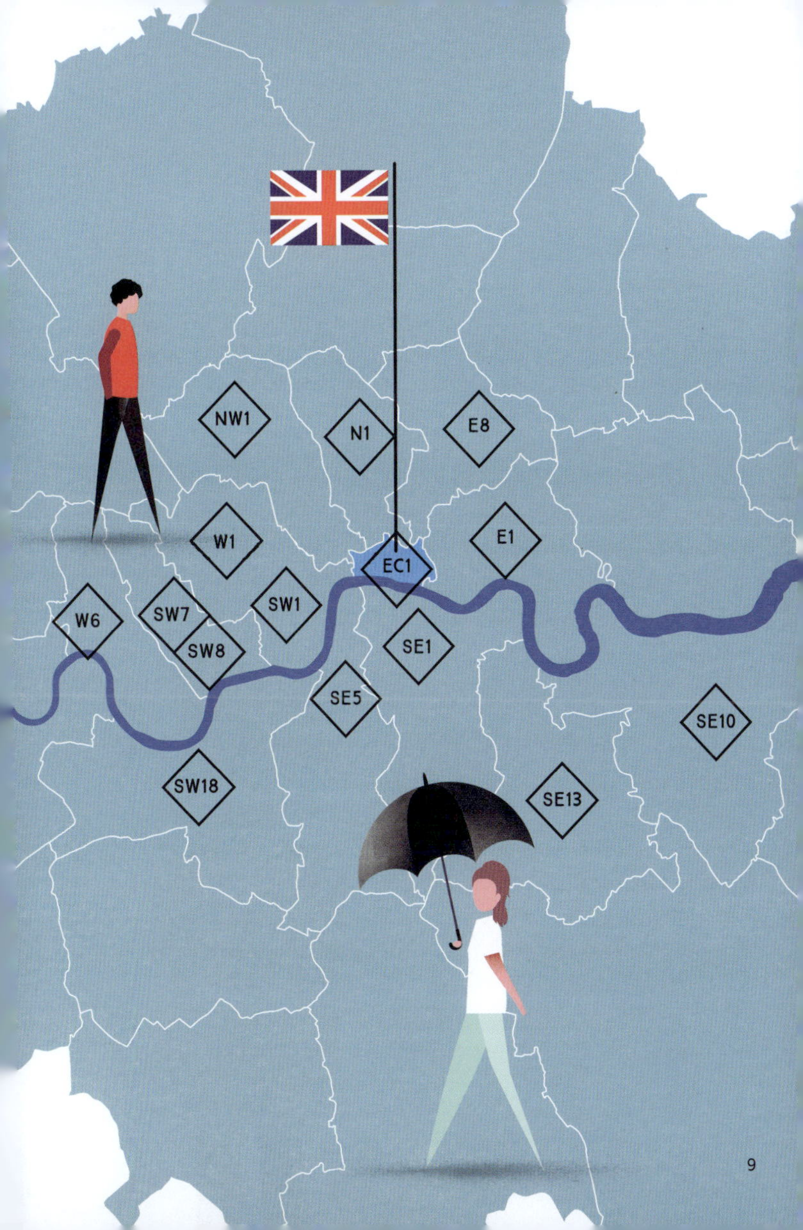
NW1
N1
E8
W1
EC1
E1
W6
SW7
SW8
SW1
SE1
SE5
SE10
SW18
SE13

Islington (N1)

Here you'll find Arsenal and the Emirates Stadium, the largest in the country. There are also plenty of boutiques as well as arts and entertainment venues.

Tower Hamlets (E1)

Home to Tower Bridge, Brick Lane, St. Katherine's Docks, and the skyscrapers and chic shopping malls of Canary Wharf: this must be one of London's most diverse boroughs.

Hackney (E8)

An area known for its young and creative community, galleries, nightlife, Hackney Empire, and London Fields. And Shoreditch, with its trendsetting vibe, bars, and restaurants.

Southwark (SE1)

This area is a must-visit for foodies because of Borough Market. Tate Modern, the Shakespeare's Globe Theatre, and the Millennium Bridge are also very worthy of your time.

Lambeth (SE1)

Mainly a residential area, but also home to the London Eye, the Southbank Centre, Brixton Market, and the infamous Leake Street (or the Banksy Tunnel).

Greenwich (SE10)

Where the prime meridian divides the western and eastern hemispheres and where Greenwich Mean Time originates. The Royal Observatory, the Royal Naval College, Greenwich Park, and the covered market are its main attractions.

Lewisham (SE13)

A residential area and home to Lewisham Market, the Horniman Museum and Gardens, and the green open spaces of Blackheath.

Westminster (SW1)

Home to the UK Government. The Houses of Parliament, Buckingham Palace, the National Gallery, and Trafalgar Square can all be found here, as well as Soho and most of the West End.

Kensington & Chelsea (SW7, W8)

Known for luxury shopping and Notting Hill, but it also houses some of the best museums in the world: the Natural History Museum, the Science Museum, and the Victoria and Albert Museum to name a few.

Wandsworth (SW18)

Very family-friendly, with vast open spaces like Battersea Park and Wandsworth Common. And the iconic Battersea Power Station.

Hammersmith & Fulham (W6)

This part of town is home to three professional football clubs: Chelsea, Fulham, and Queens Park Rangers. This is also where the annual Oxford-Cambridge boat race takes place.

Camden (NW1)

This area is loved for its alternative vibe. Here you'll find quirky shops, a buzzing market, live music, thriving nightlife, as well as old-school pubs.

UNDERGROUND

PRACTICAL INFO

TRAVEL

Don't forget your passport! Since the United Kingdom left the European Union, a passport is needed for anyone who wants to enter the UK. An ID card is no longer valid for travel to London.

Travelling by train, you will arrive at London St. Pancras International Station. It's an impressive Victorian building with a huge, curved roof and plenty of spots to eat and shop. In recent years, the surrounding King's Cross area has been developed into a desirable destination in itself. From here, you have easy access to the whole of London by public transport.

If you arrive via one of London's six airports, you need to take extra time and expense into account to travel into the city. They vary, so check your options to work out which is best for you (*tfl.gov.uk/travel-information/visiting-london/getting-to-london/london-airports*). Generally, it works out cheaper to book your tickets in advance. That applies for airport transfers as well as day trips out of town from King's Cross or one of the other railway stations (*thetrainline.com*).

Contactless payment can be used on all forms of public transport in London. Fares vary depending on the type of transport, the zones you travel in, and the time and day of travel. Payment is automatically capped; just make sure you use the same card for checking in and out throughout the day. If you don't have a debit or credit card that allows for contactless payments, the Oyster Card is a pay-as-you-go electronic smartcard which can be used to pay for all public

TRAVEL

PRACTICAL INFO

transport in London. The cost of travel remains the same. The *CityMapper* app will show you the quickest route between two destinations using London's public transport system. The *Tfl Go* app is another useful tool to plan your journeys with.

Black cabs are pricey. However, if you want to ride one to get the ultimate London experience, they can be booked in advance (*gett.com*, *free-now.com*) or hailed in the street when the yellow taxi sign is on. They have a meter indicating the fare price. Minicabs may be cheaper but check the price beforehand and only use them if they have a Transport for London license disc.

Uber boats by Thames Clippers offer a fantastic way to travel from West to East along the Thames, all the way from Putney to Greenwich. You'll experience London from a completely different perspective while travelling very efficiently. Fares depend on the zones and the distance travelled (*thamesclippers.com*).

The Santander Cycle system is run by Transport for London. There are docking stations all over the city. All you need is a debit or credit card or the app. Easy! The website shows several routes taking in the major highlights, including where to find docking stations (*tfl.gov.uk/modes/cycling/santander-cycles*). Or use the Cycle Highways to travel efficiently from one side of town to the other.

WHERE TO STAY

Accommodation in London is notoriously expensive. Youth hostels (around £50-75 per night) are obviously cheaper than hotels (at least £100). They often have kitchen facilities and communal areas, making them a great place to meet new people. Most hostels don't allow under 18s. Though it might be tempting to book more affordable rooms further out, you must keep in mind that this will involve a lot of time and money spent travelling.

Generator Hostel

37 Tavistock Pl, London WC1, staygenerator.com

Stylish hostel close to Regents Park and Covent Garden. Housed in a former police station, featuring exposed brickwork and a lot of black steel. There are chill-out areas, a restaurant, a bar, and even a dance floor.

Wombats the City Hostel

7 Dock St, London E1, wombats-hostels.com

A fun and clean hostel with all sorts of rooms. There's also a bar and a terrace with hammocks. Located next to the Tower of London and Tower Bridge, it is walking distance to Shoreditch and Brick Lane, and close to Borough Market and the South Bank.

The Mornington

2 Hurdwick Pl, London NW1, morningtoncamden.com

A female-only hostel room for up to ten people, based inside a hotel. The bathrooms are luxurious, and the atmosphere is very welcoming. With lockers, WiFi, and a TV room. Perfect for female solo travellers. Close to Camden Town.

Onefam

onefamhostels.com

The perfect hostel if you like to meet new people, as they organise lots of fun activities. On two London locations. Notting Hill is perfect for exploring Portobello Road and Hyde Park. Waterloo is great for Borough Market, the Southbank, and Big Ben.

Astor

astorhostels.com

Several excellent hostels, dotted throughout central London. The Hyde Park location is perfect for exploring some of London's major museums. The one in Victoria is great for central London. Astor Kensington is good for Notting Hill and Portobello Road, whereas Astor Museum is best for Covent Garden and the West End.

University halls

kcl.ac.uk
universityrooms.com

During the summer months several university halls offer affordable rooms. It is worth checking them out if you plan to visit during the summer break.

New Road Hotel

103 New Road, London E1,
newroadhotel.co.uk

This hotel in Whitechapel is in a perfect location to explore the East End. Rooms are small but nicely decorated, and there is a good a good on-site bar and restaurant.

The Culpeper & The Buxton

40 Commercial St, London E1, theculpeper.com
42 Osborn Street, London E1, thebuxton.co.uk

Pubs with rooms! What more do you need? Both equally attractive, very welcoming, and perfectly located in Spitalfields and Brick Lane respectively. It's a short walk to Shoreditch from here, while central London can easily be reached.

YOTEL London Shoreditch

309-317 Cambridge Heath Road, London E2,
yotel.com

This hotel offers incredible value for money. Rooms are tiny, but clean and comfortable. This area is great for urban adventures, so you won't need to travel far. But if you do, the underground is nearby.

Mama Shelter

437 Hackney Road, London E2,
mamashelter.com

Come to mama! You can sleep in small or even smaller bedrooms decorated in a funky 70s style. With a restaurant, and a bar. They often have music events lined up. Shoreditch is a short stroll, while Columbia Road Flower Market is just around the corner.

Komo Pod Hotel

12 Andre Street, London E8, booking.com/hotel/gb/komo-pod

This fresh and clean hotel has small private rooms – or pods – built into the wall like a beehive. You have to really like each other to be sharing a room. Hip and happening Hackney is at your doorstep.

Kip

2 Aspland Grove, London E8, getsomekip.com

A funky budget hotel in hip Hackney close to a tube station. An affordable option if you book with a group of friends to share a bunkbed room.

Good Hotel

Royal Victoria Dock, London E16, goodhotel.co/london

Investing all of its profits back into local communities, Good Hotel is a unique not-for-profit hotel. And it floats! The waterfront location and roof terrace offer panoramic views over the Thames. Inside it's Scandi-chic with modern rooms and a plant-based restaurant.

The Pilgrm

25 London Street, London W2, thepilgrm.com

Fresh and funky boutique hotel close to Paddington Station. Close to the West End as well as Notting Hill, with plenty of opportunities to wine and dine along the way.

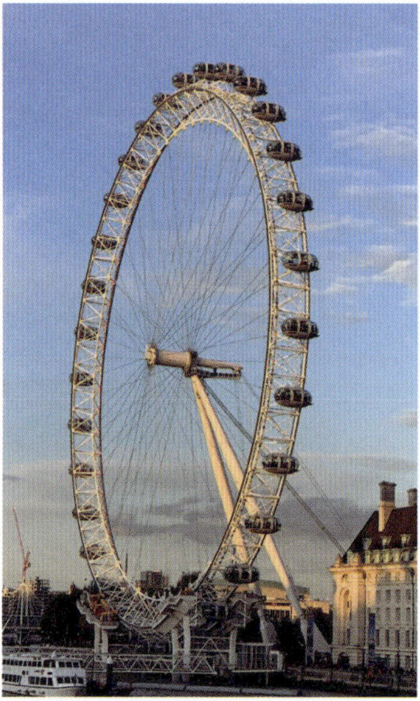

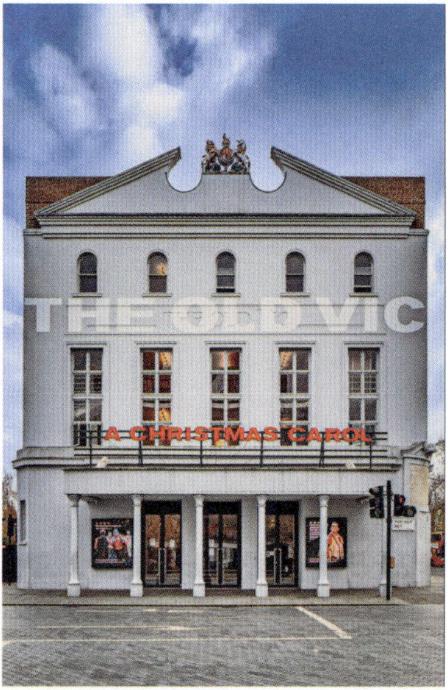
THE OLD VIC
A CHRISTMAS CAROL

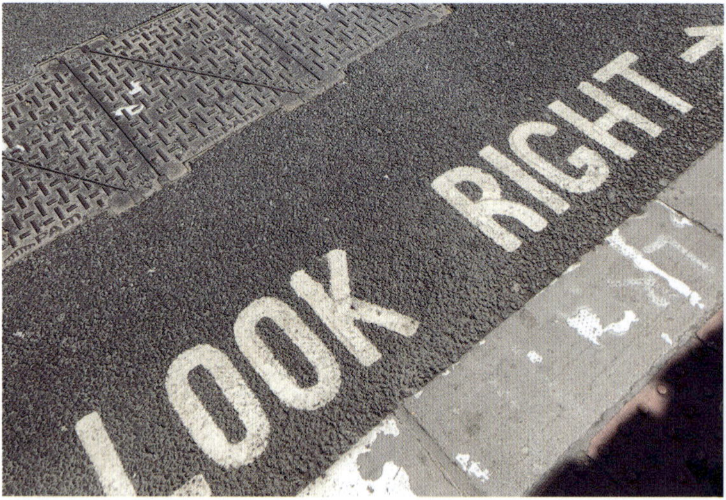
LOOK RIGHT

GOOD TO KNOW

Money

The official currency of the United Kingdom is the pound sterling (£, GBP). Most credit and debit cards as well as contactless payments are widely accepted in restaurants, bars, cafes, and shops in London. A contactless card can also be used on all public transport. Non-UK cards may incur a transaction fee, so check with your card issuer.

Charging

You probably need a travel adapter to charge your devices. The UK uses a three-pin outlet with a voltage of 230 V.

Walking

London. Is. Huge. Travelling from one side to the other is bound to take up a big chunk of your time. There is no way you can expect to see the entire city in just a few days. You're better off focusing on two or three attractions a day. Try walking from one to the other and leave some space to be surprised along the way. Walking, really, is a way of life in London. In central London, it can be faster than taking the underground, you will get to see much more of the city, and it is completely free.

Tube etiquette

Tube stations can get very crowded, especially during rush hour. To keep things moving, the escalators up and down the stations have standing and walking lanes. Stand on the right! Always! And always, always allow passengers to get off the train first.

Look left, look right

Keep in mind that the Brits drive on the left. You probably think that doesn't matter if you're not driving. Until you try crossing a road whilst looking in the wrong direction. Or riding a bicycle. Luckily 'look left' or 'look right' is often painted on the street at pedestrian crossings.

Plan & save

Most attractions are cheaper when booked ahead of time. Some, like the Harry Potter Studios and Shakespeare's Globe, get booked up months in advance. Planning is absolutely necessary if either is on your bucket list. Many hostels and hotels facilitate discounted tours and fun activities, so it is worth checking what yours has to offer.

London Pass

If you plan to visit several paid attractions, it might be worth getting a London Pass. It works out cheaper if you visit more than two attractions a day. If you plan to mainly stick to the free attractions and sightseeing, it is not value for money.

londonpass.com

Restaurants

Booking popular restaurants is advisable, especially in the high season. Good to know: most restaurants add 10-15% service charge to the final bill, especially in the touristic areas. Obviously, tipping is not needed if that is the case.

Food

There are a wide range of typically British dishes to try. The full English Breakfast, Fish & Chips, Sunday Roast and Sticky Toffee Pudding are just some traditional examples. Many consider curry to be British as well. And there is an abundance in other international food options. Make the most of those by eating your way through one of the many street-food markets. Camden Market, Borough Market, Spitalfields, Maltby Street, Broadway Market, Flat Iron Square: you are never too far away from an array of culinary delights from all over the world. It would be a crime not to visit at least one of those.

Shopping

World famous Oxford Street is a very long and very busy shopping street. It is lined with three hundred shops and receives around 500,000 visitors per day. Hardly any of them will be Londoners, though. If you really must go, try to get there on a weekday to avoid the worst crowds.

You can shop at the international chain stores as well as department stores like Harrods and Selfridges. For independent boutiques you are better off shopping in Notting Hill, Soho, Covent Garden, Islington, Camden, or Shoreditch.

Enjoy the view

The London Eye and the Shard both offer an amazing view over the city. They are both expensive too. There are plenty of options to get wonderful views for free.

- The views over the Thames from the viewing gallery at Tate Modern are incredible.
- Horizon 22, London's highest free viewing platform, needs to be booked weeks in advance.
- From the top of the beautiful park at Primrose Hill you'll get a view of the skyline.
- Watch the sun set over the London skyline from Greenwich Observatory.
- Go to Frank's Bar at Peckam Levels for a fantastic view over the city with a drink in hand.
- Book well in advance for the amazing views from Sky Garden.

West End shows

If you are looking for classic entertainment, it is hard to beat London's West End shows. Pay half of the ticket price when you buy on the day, or even just before showtime, by checking for standby tickets at the box office. Alternatively, on-the-day tickets are available to buy at the TKTS booth in Leicester Square or online. That said, the major shows need to be booked long in advance and will hardly ever have last-minute availability. If you want to save some pennies, it's best to be open minded about the shows with last-minute availability. Or look for smaller theatres further out. You might be pleasantly surprised, as quality tends to be high, anyway.

officiallondontheatre.com/tkts, lovetheatre.com, todaytix.com/london

What's on

Check what special events are happening during your stay. A concert, an exhibition, a pop-up shop, a festival, or a race, there is always something going on. Attending one of those will make you feel like a real Londoner, making your trip so much more memorable.

timeout.com, londonist.com, secretldn.com

GOOD TO KNOW

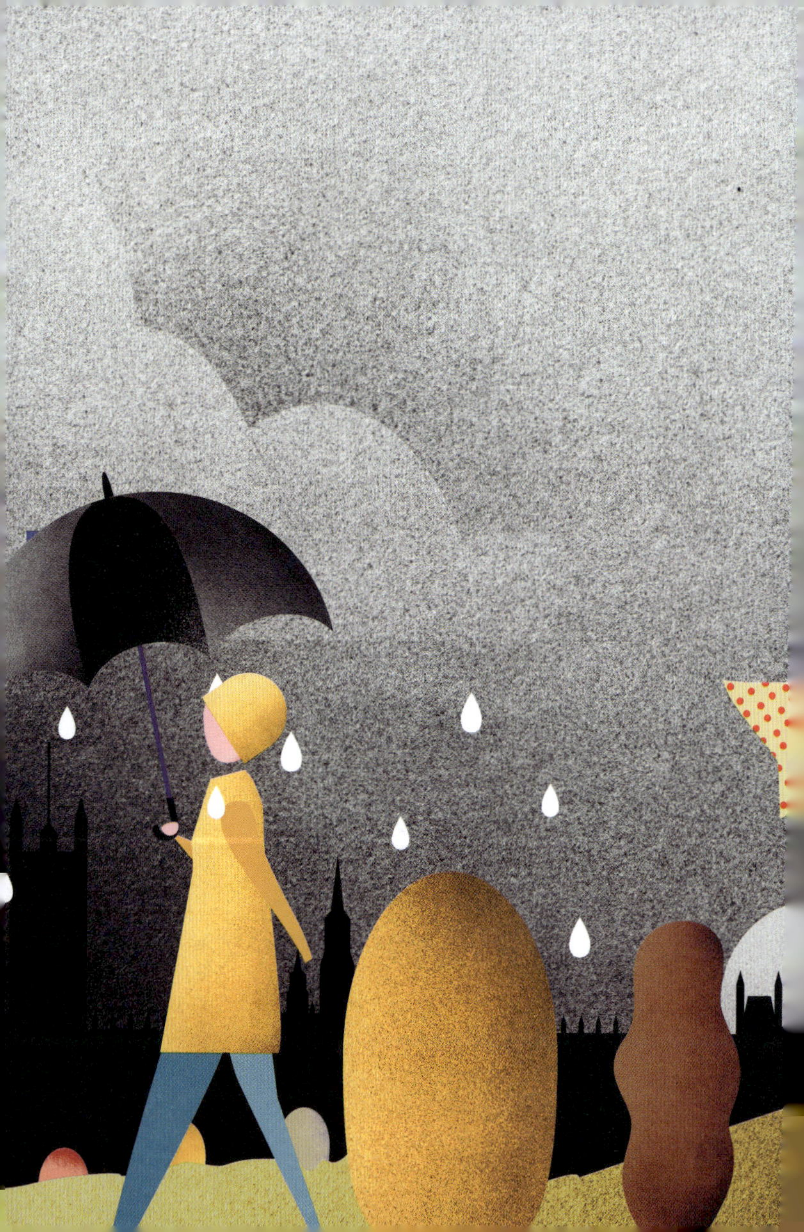

WHEN TO TRAVEL

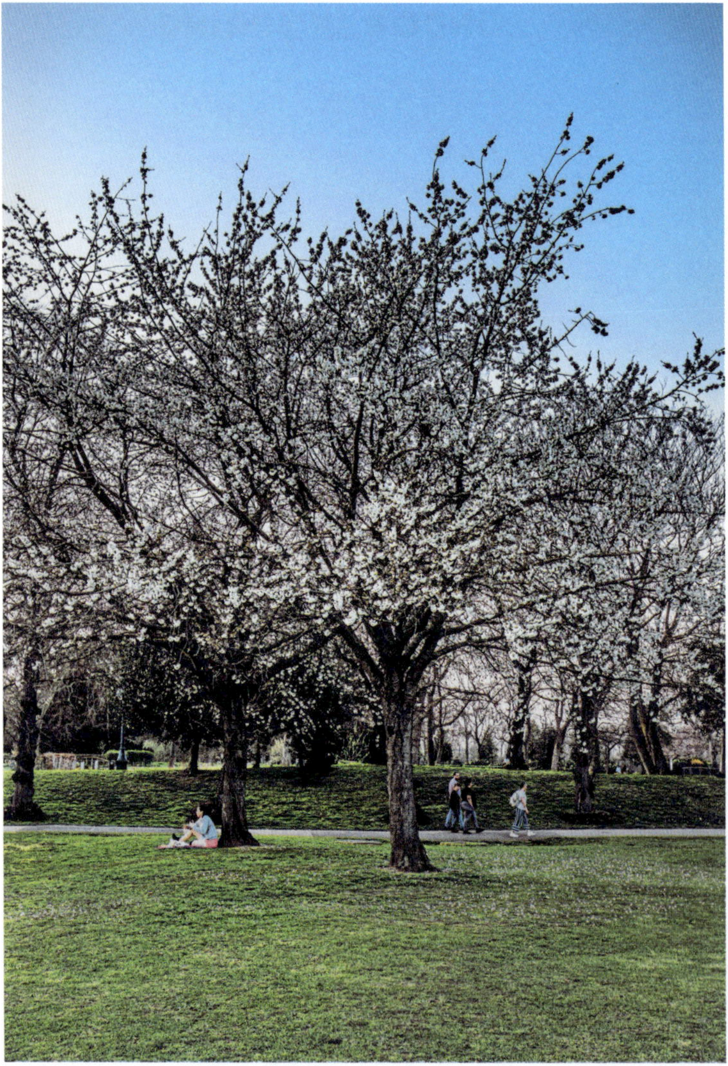

LONDON IN SPRING

Spring is a great time to visit London. The weather is picking up and you get to enjoy all the blooms and blossoms. To admire the most vibrant cherry-blossom trees, visit Kew Royal Botanic Gardens or Kyoto Garden in Holland Park. Wisteria grows abundantly in Notting Hill and Kensington. Fields of daffodils and crocuses fill the many parks. And then there's the famous Chelsea Flower Show every May, attracting keen gardeners from around the world.

May is also when London can get a bit crowded, with two bank holiday weekends in one month. Regent's Park Open Air Theatre opens for the season. The auditorium is entirely open to the elements, so come prepared! You can also join the crowds gathering on the Thames embankment for the annual Oxford-Cambridge boat race. This is a true spectacle, best enjoyed with a glass of Pimm's in hand.

A walk along the South Bank of the river Thames provides a spectacular view of London's skyline and allows you to discover some of the city's most iconic landmarks. The South Bank is also known for its street performers and musicians, ensuring there's always something entertaining to see and experience along the way. Walk from Tower Bridge all the way up to the London Eye, or vice versa. Either way, stop by Borough Market to sample some of the tasty food on offer.

LONDON IN SUMMER

The summer months are peak tourist season in London. Days are longer, and the weather tends to be pleasant. This is when London is bustling with activity. You can enjoy all sorts of outdoor events and visit open-air markets. A few major annual events take place during the summer, such as Pride in London, Notting Hill Carnival, and Wimbledon. This is also the time for plenty of music festivals. It can also get crowded, and accommodation prices tend to be higher.

If you want to go for a pleasant stroll, walk all the way from St. Katherine's Dock down to Canary Wharf. Follow the Thames Path as it winds its way along the shores of the river. You will pass some very enjoyable riverside pubs along the way, like Prospect of Whitby, Captain Kidd, and Town of Ramsgate.

You could also have a picnic in one of the many parks or go on long bike rides through the city. Catch a play at Shakespeare's Globe or see the sun setting over the skyline from Primrose Hill. Hop on one of the Uber Boats, functioning as river busses connecting East and West London. Jump aboard to visit Greenwich, marvel at its amazing Royal Naval College, and enjoy the green open spaces. The possibilities are endless.

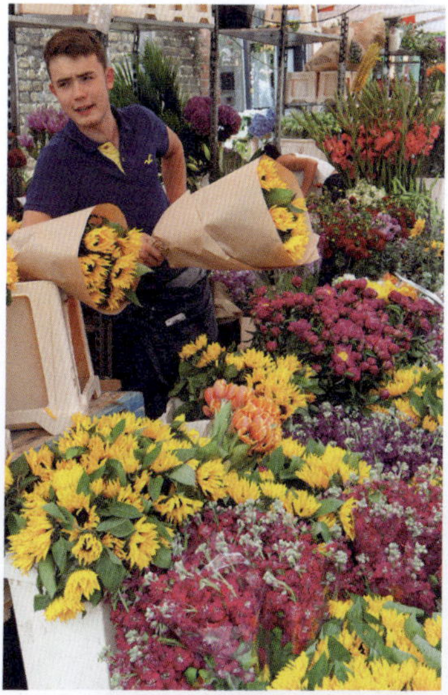

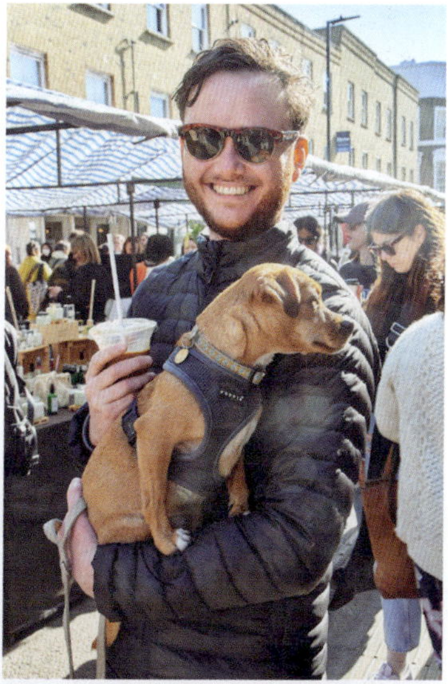

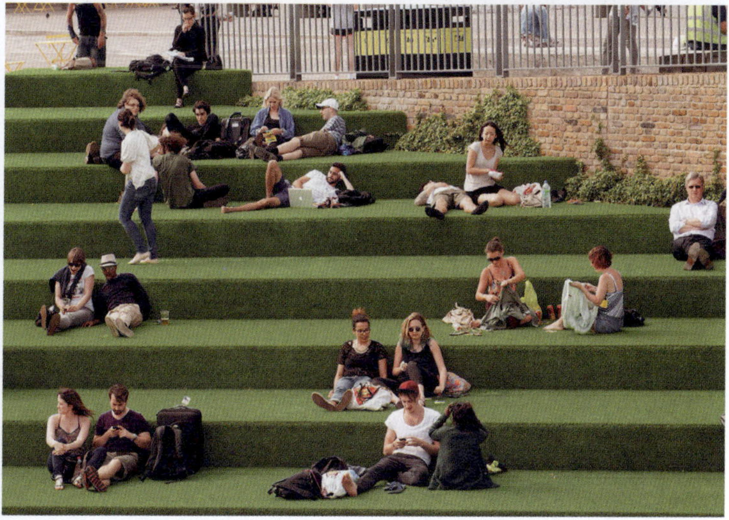

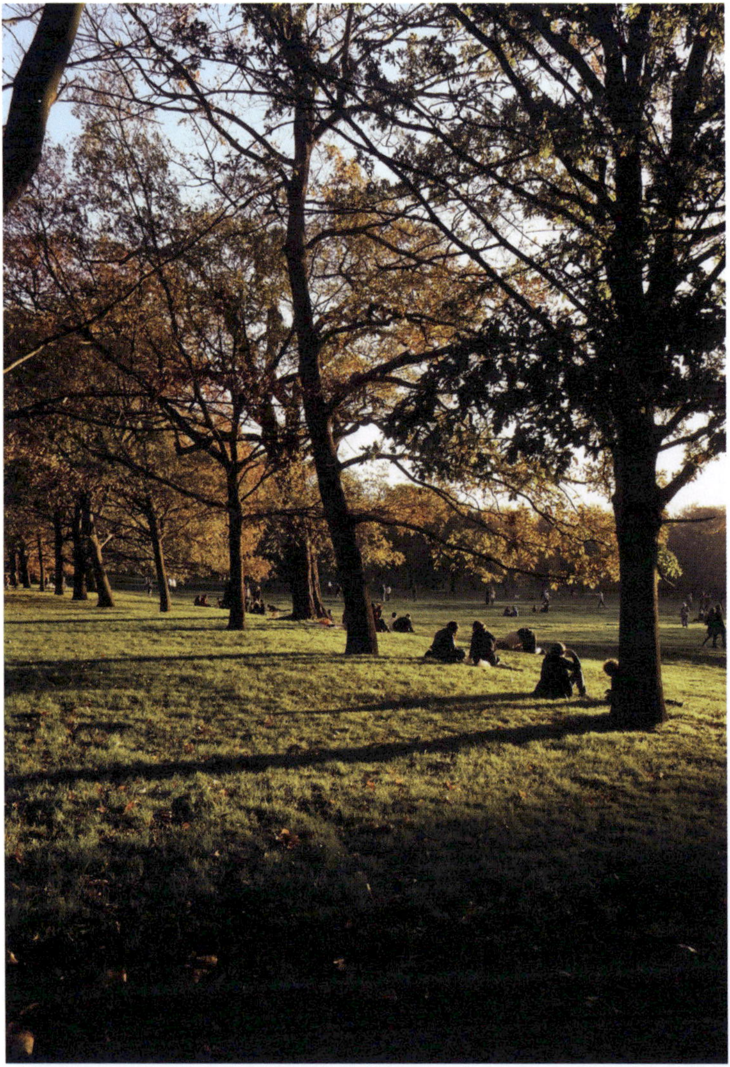

LONDON IN AUTUMN

Autumn can bring all seasons in one day, when it is simultaneously too hot and too cold for a coat, with some rain-showers thrown in for good measure. When staying indoors is the best remedy, you could catch a film at the BFI during the London Film Festival. Another annual event in London's calendar is the Totally Thames Festival along with the city-wide programme of events to commemorate Black History Month. In October, you can purchase an original work of art at the Affordable Art Fair in Battersea. For Halloween, you can take a graveyard walk through Highgate Cemetery, a Jack the Ripper tour in Whitechapel, or a ghostly tour around London Bridge. The fifth of November is Bonfire Night, so be prepared for an abundance of fireworks.

It's also a great time to explore London's many parks. A perfect autumn day in London would include a brisk walk in one of its many green open spaces, followed by a freshly brewed beer in a local pub. Hampstead Heath is particularly beautiful this time of year. Or walk the Bermondsey Beer Mile. Start at Southwark Brewing and take your pick from around twenty breweries along the way. Alternatively, you can get away from the crowds and walk from Camden Market to Little Venice along the Regent's Canal. This is always a pleasure, but it has a certain charm this time of year.

LONDON IN WINTER

In winter, Londoners like to head to the theatre. Apart from it being a British tradition, many new shows are launched in the season. Classics like *Les Miserables* and *Phantom of the Opera*, or the latest productions starring world-famous actors: there is a show for everyone. Go ice skating at one of the many ice rinks. The biggest ice rink can be found in Hyde Park, the prettiest at Somerset House, and the highest is Skylight Ice Rink on the rooftop of Tobacco Dock. Or visit a light festival. Enchanted Eltham, Kenwood and Kew Gardens are further out but worth the effort.

In the lead up to Christmas there simply is no better place to be. The entire city is transformed into a winter wonderland. Christmas lights, Christmas markets, and mulled wine whichever way you turn. Oxford Street, Carnaby Street, Regent Street, Covent Garden, and Mayfair are completely illuminated; central London is aglow. Shop for presents at the famous department stores, all dressed up for Christmas. Go to Liberty's for the pretty prints, Fortnum & Mason for foodie presents, Hamleys for toys, and Selfridges for gadgets and streetwear.

The Lunar New Year, celebrated between the end of January and early February, draws big crowds to London's Chinatown for a big celebration. And last but not least, this is the perfect time to visit some of the amazing and free museums.

VINTER

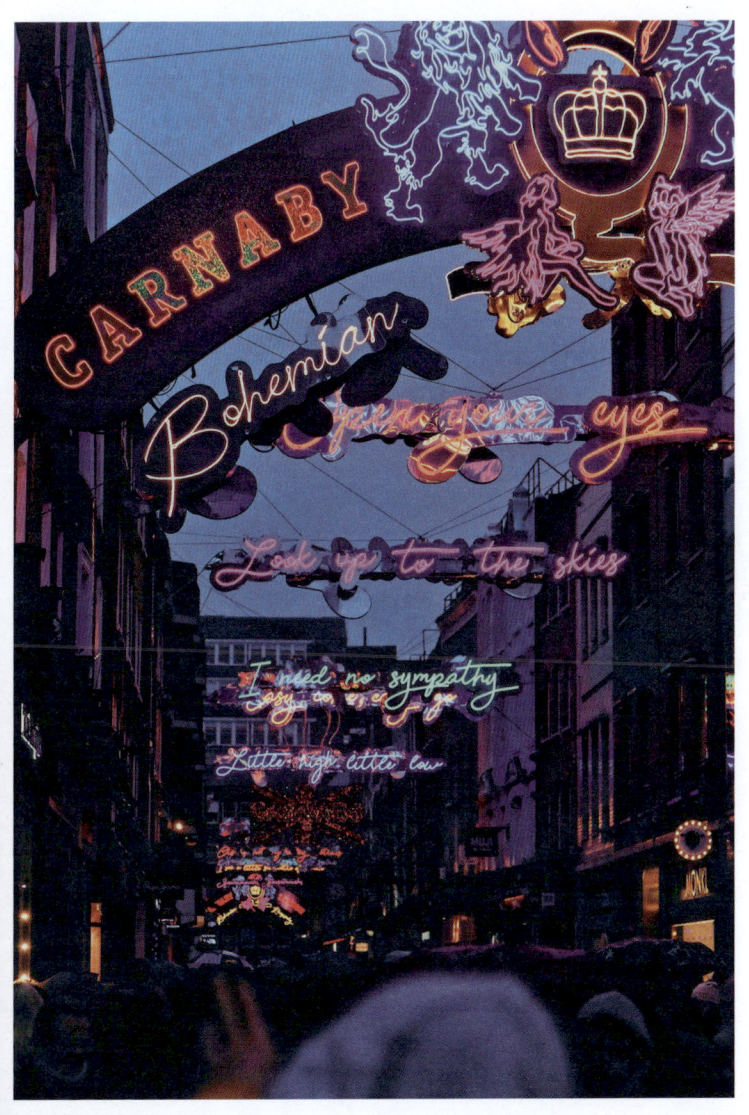

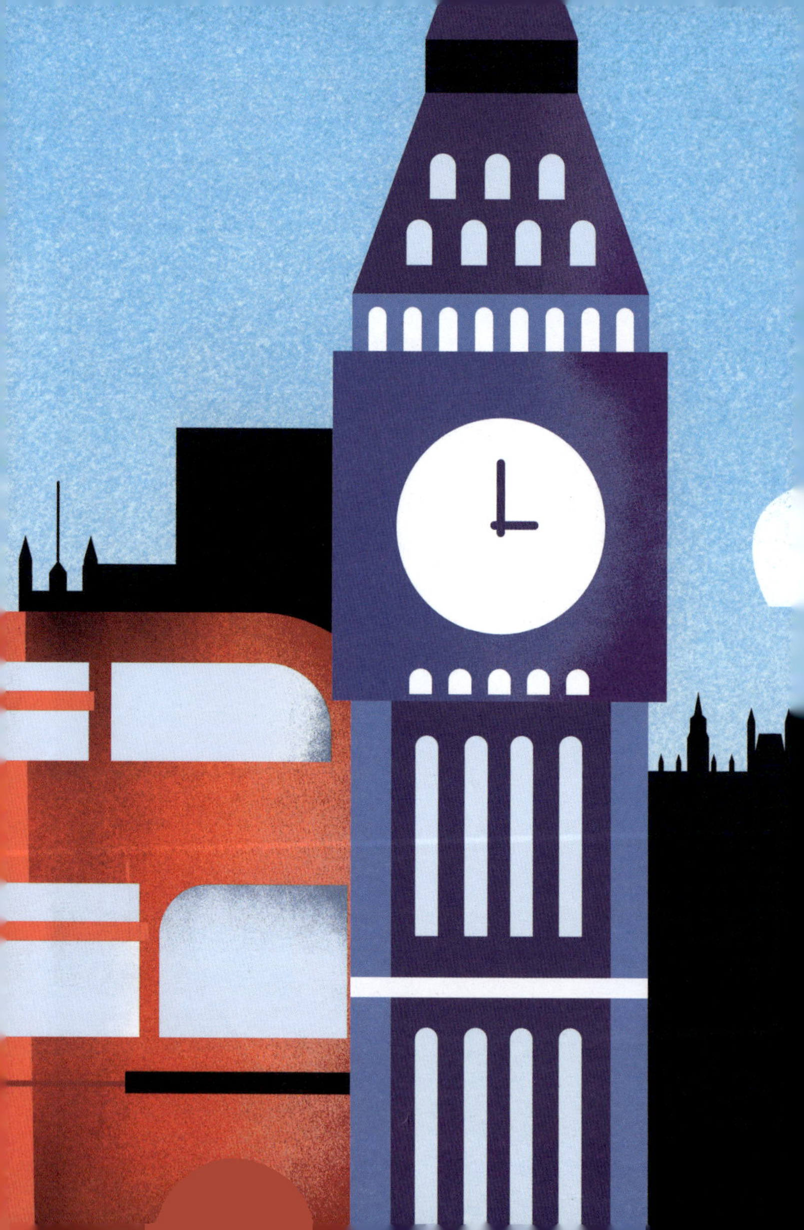

LONDON LIFE

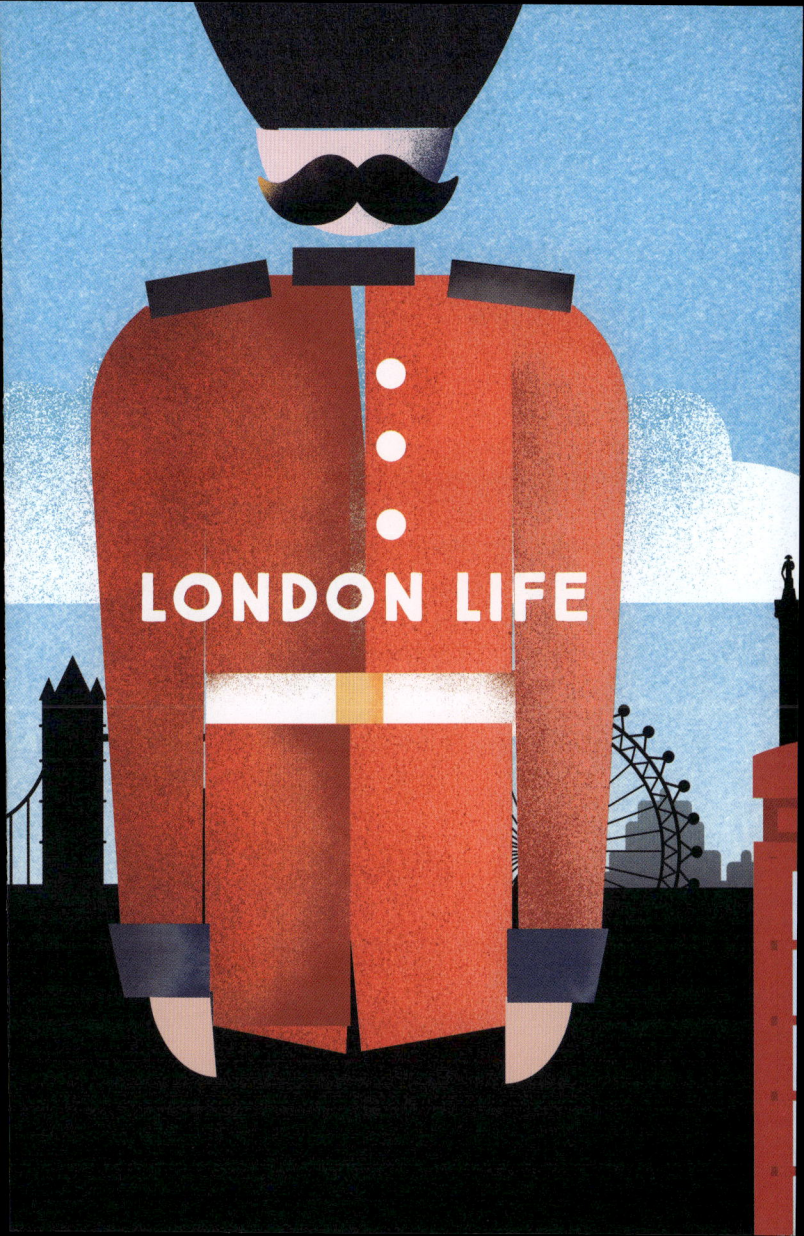

HISTORY

London's origins

The origin of Londinium, as it was named by the ancient Romans, dates back two millennia. London was loved by the Romans because of its access to mainland Europe. The city was founded in 43 CE at the narrowest point of the river, enabling the Romans to trade along the river. Eventually, they built a bridge over the Thames at that point. It may be hard to imagine, but Roman London was as big as Hyde Park is today.

Beefeaters

The notable Yeomen Warders are known for their red uniforms with gold decorations. Locals call the ceremonial guards of the Tower of London 'Beefeaters'. The story goes that the nickname comes from the fact that the Yeomen Warders used to receive their wages in the form of meats, including beef.

The Great Fire

Sunday, 2nd September 1666 was a dark day in London history. The wooden houses, the long, dry summer, and the scarcity of water were the ideal conditions for the start of a fire. It started in a bakery on Pudding Lane and resulted in the entire city catching fire. The Great Fire resulted in an immense loss of life as well as 13,200 homes. A quote from the diary of resident Samuel Pepys: 'Lord! what sad sight it was by moonlight to see, the whole City almost on fire, that you might see it plain at Woolwich, as if you were by it.'

Theatres

With Shakespeare as a former resident, it is not surprising that there are hundreds of theatres in London. Shakespeare used the capital as a backdrop for his most famous works. His fans should catch a play at The Globe: a replica of Shakespeare's original theatre. Shakespeare's Globe, like all theatres in his time, has no roof since the actors needed daylight for their plays. You need a bit of imagination, as every scene starts with the actor stating the time, location, and weather in the play. You might not have realised, but theatre has not always been a legal activity in London. Between 1642 and 1660, large fines were given out when plays were performed, but it was still practised in secret. It shows the importance of theatre, then and still to this day. The West End is currently the beating theatre heart of London.

London Underground

To ease congestion in the streets, London introduced the world's first metro line in 1863. The Metropolitan Railway started off with a steam locomotive, covering passengers and stations in black, sticky soot. The switch to electricity was a major improvement. During World War II, the underground stations served as bomb shelters during air raids. The Underground nowadays has eleven lines covering 402km, serving 272 stations and handling up to five million passenger journeys every day.

Royal Observatory Greenwich

This is one of the few places in the world where you can stand in the Eastern Hemisphere and in the Western Hemisphere at the same time. The prime meridian was assigned here in 1884. And it runs straight through the building and can

The Coronation
King
Charles III
6th May
2023
Original
head&shoulders
smooth & silky
head&shoulders
clean & balanced
head&shoulders
dry scalp care
seda
seda
P.B.
LONDON
KEEP
CALM

be recognised by the metal strip on the ground. Greenwich Mean Time is the yearly average (or 'mean') of the time each day when the sun crosses the Prime Meridian at the Royal Observatory. It is a UNESCO World Heritage site, not only because of the Greenwich Meridian, but also for the museum, where you learn everything about astronomy. Here you can also admire the Great Equatorial Telescope. This historic telescope offered astronomers one hundred years ago a new perspective on the world.

Olympic Games

London was the first city to host the Olympic Games three times: in 1908, 1948, and 2012. The 2012 Games resulted in what is now the Queen Elizabeth Olympic Park. To build this impressive park, two million tonnes of soil were cleaned of the pollution left behind by two hundred years of coal barges and railway works. It has improved the entire area around it. The park is now full of adventure and activities. The London Aquatics Centre is spectacular if you want to have a swim pretending to be an Olympic athlete.

Royal Family

The house of Windsor, the royal house of the United Kingdom, succeeded the house of Hanover in 1901 on the death of its last monarch, Queen Victoria. In 1917, during WW I, the family changed its name from the German Saxe-Coburg-Gotha to Windsor in an attempt to erase all English ties with Germany. King George V, King Charles' great-grandfather, was the first monarch of Windsor. The British royal house, with icons like Queen Elizabeth II, Princess Diana and King Charles is world famous. Next in line to the throne is Prince

William. In 2020 his brother, Prince Harry, together with his wife Meghan stepped down as senior royals due to the ongoing media intrusion. The official residence of the monarchs is Buckingham Palace. When the king is present, the royal standard flies on the middle pavilion.

Bobbies

London police officers are referred to as Bobbies. This term originates from Robert 'Bobby' Peel. In the 1920s there was so much chaos and crime in the city that police forces were desperately needed. Sir Robert Peel, Minister of Internal Affairs, installed a professional civilian police force that turned out very successful in reducing crime rates. His nickname Bobby is still used as an unofficial term for a police officer.

World War II

Being the largest city in the world at the start of WW II, London was one of the favourite targets of the Luftwaffe (German Air Force). The German's Blitzkrieg tactic was to conquer as much territory as quickly as possible. Winston Churchill, who served as Conservative Prime Minister at the time, was an inspirational statesman. Despite the many losses and incredible damage, he led Britain to victory. You can visit the fascinating Churchill War Rooms in Westminster, where Churchill was headquartered during the war, to gain some insight into those turbulent times.

City of Parks

Every single neighbourhood in London has at least one park. Actually, one third of the city consists of parks. It is no coincidence that many of them

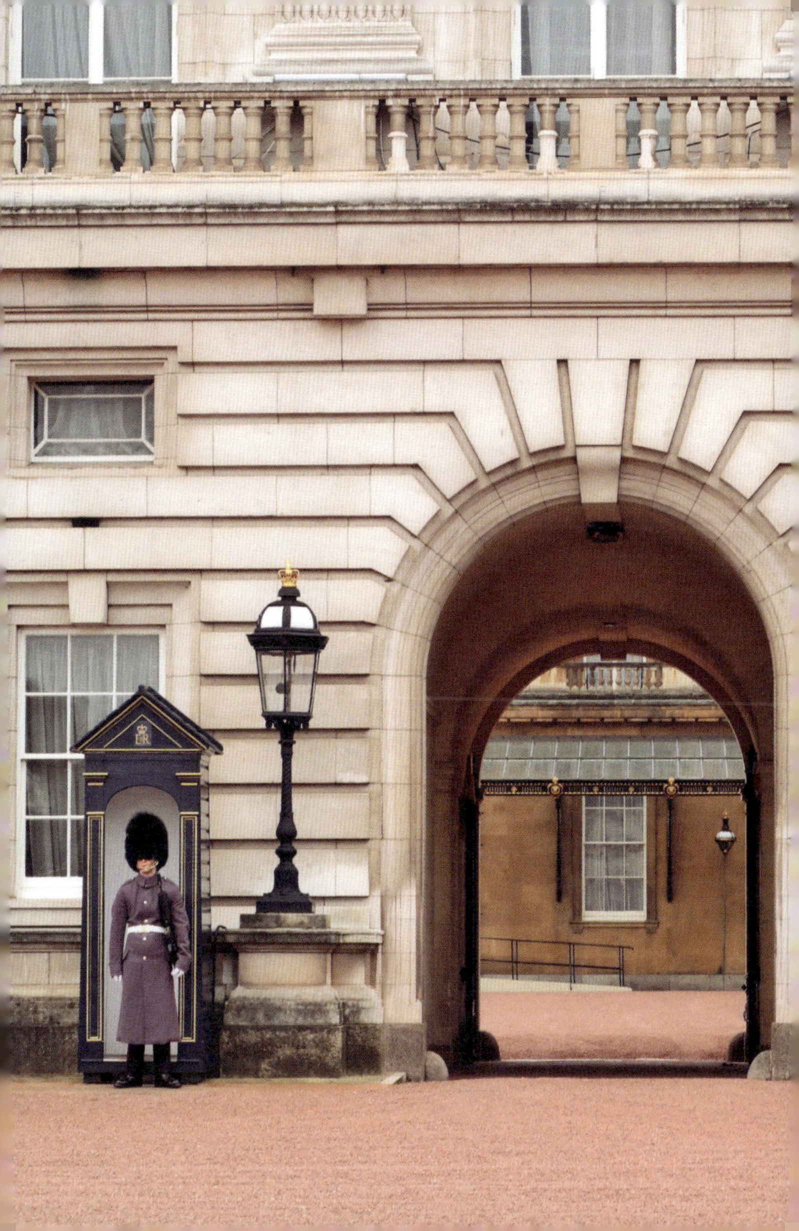

are close to royal palaces. Several parks can be traced back to King Henry VIII in the 1500s, who rode and hunted in Greenwich Park and Richmond Park. He also turned the land which now makes up Hyde Park, Kensington Gardens, and Regent's Park into hunting grounds. He built the palace of Whitehall, with gardens that are now known as St. James's Park and Green Park. Over the centuries that followed, generations of British monarchs made their mark on the green spaces. Gradually, they opened to the public. Hyde Park was the first and by the 1800s all parks were open to everyone. During the Industrial Revolution in the 19th century, London and its population grew rapidly. To keep residents healthy and happy, more and more parks were included in the city planning. These parks are seen as the 'green lungs' of the city.

Brexit

The question that lingered for years: should Britain remain or exit the European Union? On 31st January 2020, Brexit became fact and Britain left the European Union. The Brexit campaign's slogan *Take back control* attached great value to British sovereignty. The British Empire once was the largest empire in the world. And they were never conquered during WW II. This contributed to the need for sovereignty among some of the British. However, the opinion in the country was divided and ultimately a small majority of 52% voted to leave the EU. The majority of Londoners voted to remain.

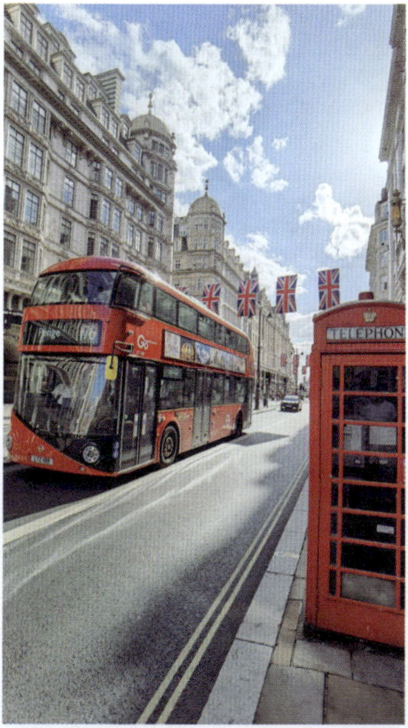
TELEPHON

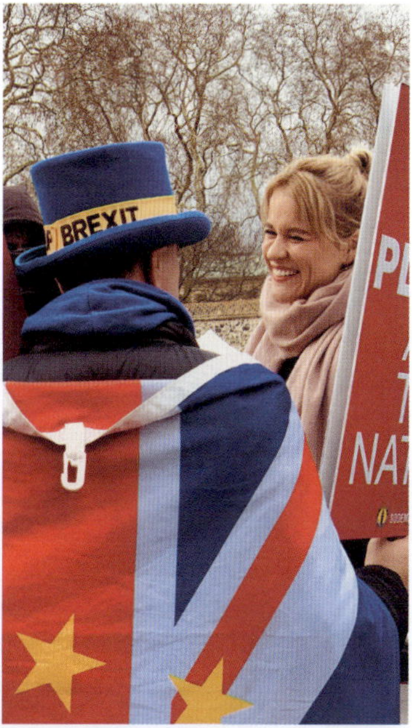
BREXIT

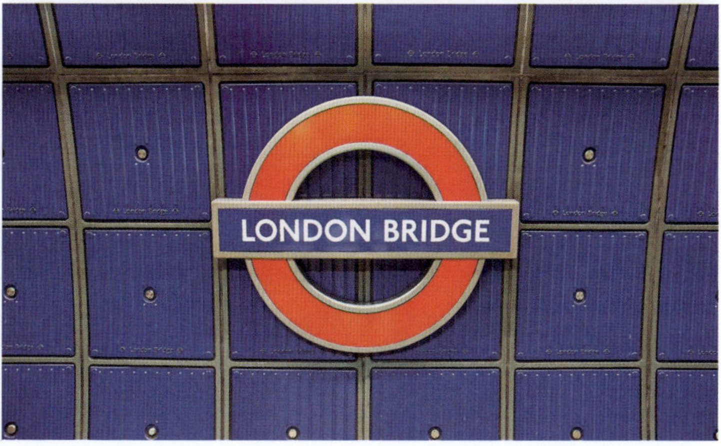
LONDON BRIDGE

SIGHTSEEING

Tower of London

London EC3, hrp.org.uk

Built in 1078 CE, the Tower of London has almost 1,000 years of history. Learn about the gruesome details, marvel at the glistening Crown Jewels, and learn about the famous ravens. It's not cheap to enter, but it is the number one sight in London for good reason. Beefeaters are great storytellers, so a tour is recommended. Booking in advance will save you a few pounds.

St. Paul's Cathedral

St. Paul's Churchyard, London EC4, stpauls.co.uk

Designed by Sir Christopher Wren in the late 17th century, St. Paul's Cathedral is still a working church. The iconic building in the City of London can be visited for services (free of charge) or for sightseeing and all sorts of events.

Trafalgar Square

Trafalgar Square, London WC2, london.gov.uk

Together with Piccadilly Circus and Leicester Square, Trafalgar Square is one of the most famous squares in London. Trafalgar Square was opened to the public in 1844 and is the heart of London. Here, rallies and marches take place, tens of thousands of people celebrate the New Year, and locals meet for all sorts of events such as open-air cinema and Christmas celebrations. It is dominated by 52-metre-tall Nelson's

↓ TRAFALGAR SQUARE

↓ ST. PAUL'S CATHEDRAL

↓ TRAFALGAR SQUARE

↓ DOWNING STREET

Column and guarded by four bronze lion statues. It is surrounded by majestic buildings like the National Gallery and the church St. Martin-in-the-Fields.

Buckingham Palace

London SW1, rct.uk, householddivision.org.uk

Since 1837, Buckingham Palace has been the official London residence of the UK's monarch. It is now the administrative headquarters of the king. Every summer, The State Rooms in the palace, normally used for state visits and other big events, are open to visitors. The Changing of the Guard is world famous. The ceremony takes place every day and involves the old guard handing over duties to the new guard, accompanied by music and marching. This historic tradition is free to watch.

Westminster Abbey

Dean's Yard, London SW1, westminster-abbey.org

The abbey has been a working religious site for almost 1,000 years. On 13 October 1163, Edward the Confessor's body was moved to a special shrine within the abbey. Since then, royal weddings, coronations, and burials have taken place here, in the saint's presence. Kings and Queens, important scientists, poets, and musicians are buried in Westminster Abbey. In June 2018 the ashes of physicist Stephen Hawking were the last to be interred in the abbey. Attending a service is free of charge.

Houses of Parliament

*London SW1,
parliament.uk*

The Palace of Westminster houses the Parliament of the United Kingdom. People often call it the Houses of Parliament, as the House of Commons and the House of Lords reside here. Part of the palace is the Elizabeth Tower, which you might know as Big Ben. Officially, Big Ben is the name of one of the clock's bells.

10 Downing Street

10 Downing Street, London SW1, gov.uk

This must be the most famous front door in London. 10 Downing Street is the official residence as well as the office of the British Prime Minister. There is no access to the house, you can only take a peek through a gate at the side of the road.

The British Library

96 Euston Road, London NW1, bl.uk

This national library of the United Kingdom, and one of the world's largest libraries. Its collections include over 150 million items in more than 400 languages. This includes books, magazines, manuscripts, maps, music scores, newspapers, historical documents, photographs, prints, drawings, and sound recordings. You can take a tour or visit one of the exhibitions. To study or read in the British Library, you must be a resident.

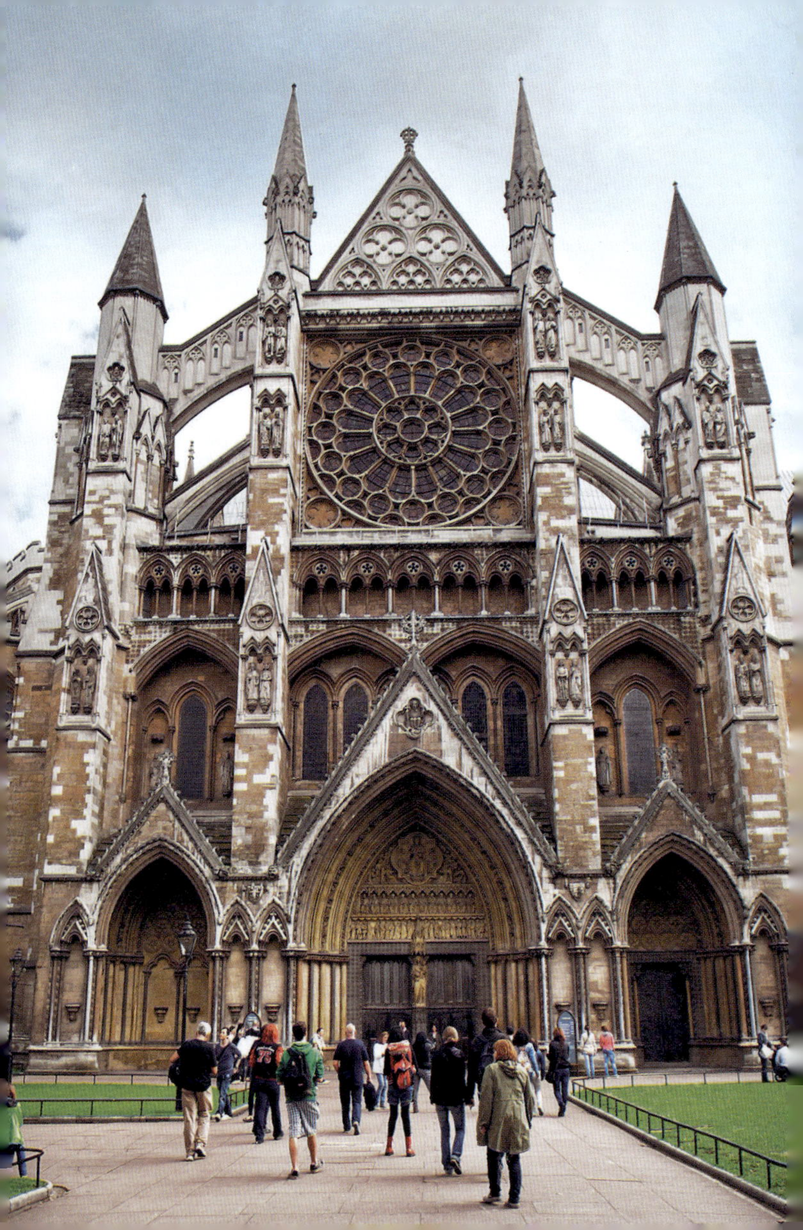

↓ TOWER BRIDGE

MUSEUMS

London is home to some of the best museums and galleries in the world. Visiting all of them is impossible. Most are completely free, but you often need to book online, so plan ahead if you can. We'll list some of the best.

British Museum

Great Russell Street, London WC1, britishmuseum.org

Although not uncontroversial, The British Museum covers the whole of human history. It houses one of the largest permanent collections in the world. A staggering eight million artefacts in total! The exhibits include highlights such as the Rosetta Stone and Egyptian mummies.

National Gallery

Trafalgar Square, London WC2, nationalgallery.org.uk

The National Gallery, not to be confused with the National Portrait Gallery, is one of the world's greatest. Filled to the brims with works from the 13th to the mid-20th century, including masterpieces by Leonardo da Vinci, Michelangelo, Vincent van Gogh, and Auguste Renoir.

Whitechapel Gallery

77-82 Whitechapel High Street, London E1, whitechapelgallery.org

This mall gallery hosts enticing temporary exhibitions rather than maintain a permanent one. It hosts edgy exhibitions of contemporary art, loved by art students. It staged the first UK shows by the likes of Jackson Pollock, Mark Rothko, and Frida Kahlo. The gallery's exhibitions change every couple of months, and it frequently hosts live music events, talks, and film screenings. There is a nice café and an excellent bookshop.

The Museum of the Home

136 Kingsland Road, London E2, museumofthehome.org.uk

This museum was originally an 18th century alms-house and hospital for London's East End underclass. It is now a museum designed to illustrate typical London home life from the 1600s to modern day. A series of sitting and living rooms is displayed to show how daily life in London has changed throughout the centuries. It gives an insight into the life of a typical Londoner, offering a counterbalance to the affluent Royal history presented by London's better known tourist sites.

↓ VICTORIA AND ALBERT MUSEUM

Tate Britain

Millbank, London SW1, tate.org.uk/visit/tate-britain

Tate Britain, not to be confused with Tate Modern, opened in 1892. Its focus is on British art from 1500 to the present. It includes pieces from William Blake, Thomas Gainsborough, and John Constable, as well as modern pieces from the likes of Francis Bacon and Henry Moore. The main attraction are the works of JMW Turner in the Clore Gallery.

Tate Modern

Bankside, London SE1, tate.org.uk/visit/tate-modern

This museum for modern and contemporary art, not to be mistaken for Tate Britain, is worth a visit for its building alone. The former power station is standing tall at the banks of the Thames. You'll find all sorts of temporary and permanent exhibitions, enjoy the view from the viewing gallery, and shop at the excellent museum shop.

Tower Bridge

Tower Bridge Road, London SE1, towerbridge.org.uk

A trip to London is not complete without crossing the iconic Tower Bridge. Its steel construction was considered spectacular when it opened in 1894. You can enter the upper level and walk along the glass floor, which isn't free, but still affordable.

Shakespeare's Globe

21 New Globe Walk, London SE1 shakespearesglobe.com, thestageshoreditch.com

A reconstruction of the original Globe Theatre (1599), the theatre that Shakespeare wrote many of his plays for. You can join in a tour or watch a play. Book well in advance and you could bag yourself a £5 standing ticket. If there is no availability left, quickly make your way to the spanking new Museum of Shakespeare on the site of The Curtain Playhouse, in Shoreditch.

The Shard

*32 London Bridge Street,
London SE1,
the-shard.com*

The glass skyscraper, spiking high into London's sky, is immediately recognisable. At 310 metres, it is the tallest building in the UK. It houses offices, apartments, a luxury hotel with several restaurants, and a viewing gallery on the 72nd floor. It is by far the highest observation platform in the British capital. From here, you can take in 360-degree views of the city and beyond. But it's not cheap. You could spend the same amount of money on a few drinks at bar Gong on the 52nd floor (a minimum spend of £30 each). But you must book and dress up for the occasion.

↓ TATE BRITAIN

White Cube Bermondsey

144-152 Bermondsey Street, London SE1, whitecube.com

White Cube is a contemporary art gallery with spaces in London, Hong Kong, Paris, New York, and Seoul. It was founded by Jay Jopling, who made his reputation in the 1990s by exhibiting new artists such as Tracey Emin and Damien Hirst. It is one of two galleries in London, and the largest of the White Cube galleries. The former warehouse's huge exhibition spaces are perfect to showcase monumental pieces and large installations.

National Maritime Museum

Romney Road, London SE10, rmg.co.uk

The National Maritime Museum in Greenwich focusses on Britain's historic role as a naval superpower. There are interactive displays, curious nautical items, and a record-breaking speedboat.

↓ THE DESIGN MUSEUM

↓ NATURAL HISTORY MUSEUM

Old Royal Naval College

London SE10, ornc.org

The symmetrical buildings of the Old Royal Naval College in Greenwich are absolutely stunning. Wander through 600 years of history, admire the painted hall, or join a Blockbuster Film Tour. From Napoleon to The Crown, some of the world's biggest blockbusters were filmed here.

Queen's House

Romney Road, London SE10, rmg.co.uk

On the same grounds you'll find the beautiful Queen's House. When it was completed in the 1630s, it was at the cutting edge of architecture. Tickets are free but need to be booked.

The Royal Observatory

Blackheath Avenue, London SE10, rmg.co.uk

On the top of the hill in Greenwich Park, the Royal Observatory is standing proud. It is home to the prime meridian (longitude 0° 0' 0"). A ticket gives you access to Flamsteed House (named after the first Royal Astronomer) as well as the Meridian Courtyard, where you can stand with one foot in the eastern and one in the western hemisphere. You can also see the Great Equatorial Telescope inside the observatory and explore space and time in the Weller Astronomy Galleries.

Saatchi Gallery

Duke of York's HQ, King's Road, London SW3, saatchigallery.com

The Saatchi Gallery was opened by Charles Saatchi in 1985. It showcases contemporary works of art in a spectacular exhibition space. Exhibitions focus on both young artists and international artists new to the UK. The aim is to inspire a passion for contemporary art in all. There is a range of temporary exhibitions and events, a bookshop, and a café.

↓ NATURAL HISTORY MUSEUM

↓ VICTORIA AND ALBERT MUSEUM

Natural History Museum

Cromwell Road, London SW7. nhm.ac.uk

The Natural History Museum grabs your attention from the moment you enter. The huge central hall is dominated by a giant blue whale skeleton hanging from the ceiling. Wander through the different halls, filled with extraordinary displays of extinct species, dinosaur fossils, a moon rock, and much more.

LONDON LIFE

Science Museum

Exhibition Road, London SW7, sciencemuseum.org.uk

This amazing museum showcases the history of science, from the earliest technology to space travel, and from medicine to the best videogames of the past fifty years. You can learn about all the discoveries that helped change the course of human history. Visitors of all ages will love this museum.

Victoria and Albert Museum

Cromwell Road, London SW7, vam.ac.uk

The V&A Museum is the largest museum in the world for arts, design, and performance. 2.7 Million works are housed in this impressive building. Marvel at Tippoo's *Tiger and Auguste*, Rodin's *Cybele*, as well as fabrics, fashion, ceramics, contemporary design and much, much more. The museum shop is also worth your time.

The Photographers Gallery

16-18 Ramillies Street, London W1, thephotographersgallery.org.uk

London's largest public gallery completely devoted to photography. There are six galleries spanning five floors. Since 1997, it has awarded the prestigious Deutsche Börse Photography Foundation Prize. Its café is quite nice and the shop stocks an amazing selection of photography books.

The Design Museum

224-238 Kensington High Street, London W8, designmuseum.org

At its stunning new location in Holland Park (the previous site of the Commonwealth Institute), this museum focuses on the role of design in all its forms in everyday life. That includes fashion, architecture, industrial and graphic design, and much more. The interior is an ode to design by itself and the museum shops are very tempting.

STREET ART

When it comes to street art, the streets of London form the best canvas. One thing is certain; its walls, street signs, and doors are not sacred. They are not enclosed, nor protected. You can visit an area once and then return later only to see completely different works. Street art in London is constantly evolving, very diverse, sometimes messy, and often provocative. Local artists like to use the medium to raise awareness about relevant issues, turning it into so much more than art. It is a very powerful form of expression too.

Wander the streets and alleys in East London and you're certainly in for a treat. Visit Leake Street tunnel and you could catch works in the making. Go to South London for large scale pieces, or marvel at the impressive works around Camden. There is so much to see, it is hard to decide where to go first.

East London

East London's Shoreditch and Hackney are brimming with street art, making it impossible to miss. You can join a street art tour or discover it by yourself. 70 Holywell Lane in Shoreditch is a good place to start. The colourful mural is made by legendary French street artist Thierry Noir, known as the first to paint on the Berlin Wall. There's a lot more street art to be found further down the road. Princelet Street, Hanbury Street, Corbet Place, Brick Lane, Dray Walk, Wheeler Street, Sclater Street, Whitby Street ... the list is endless.

Some of Banksy's work can be seen in Rivington Street.

A visit to Pure Evil Gallery in Leonard Street should be on your list too. In the gallery, you can see Pure Evil's work along with that of other street artists. At the corner of Buxton Street and Brick Lane, the wall is plastered with posters and stickers. This is one of London's most popular spots for paste-up street art.

From the moment you exit Hackney Wick station, you'll be treated to vibrant art on the walls. The Lord Napier pub is covered in art and worth checking out. Other streets to wander are Holywell Lane, King John Court, New Inn Yard, and the streets around Broadway Market.

Leake Street Tunnel

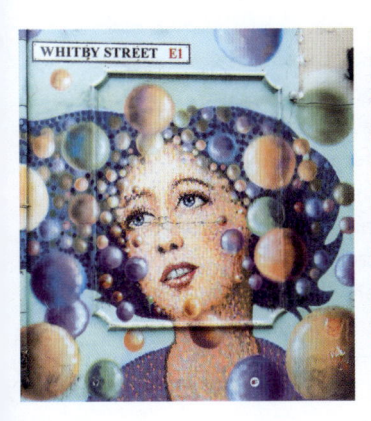

This was one of the first in London's graffiti scene. Back in 2007, Banksy organised a graffiti festival in this tunnel, to which he invited some of his most talented friends. Together, they transformed a gloomy tunnel into a piece of art. Today this is London's largest legal wall, so anyone can freely spray. This means that quality tends to vary, but also that you are very likely to witness a piece of the action.

South London

There are several areas in South London where street art is slowly taking over. Brixton makes for a good starting point. It is a cultural melting pot, that has given rise to a unique and diverse street art scene. David Bowie, who was born in Brixton, has his own mural opposite Brixton underground station. It was painted in 2013, but since his death in 2016, it has become a permanent shrine. Walk along Electric Avenue and wander through the area to discover many more amazing pieces. Many of Brixton's graffiti pieces carry social and political messages. Most are illuminated after dark. A good combo with the vibrant street-food scene. If you are hungry for more, Peckham, Penge, and Lewisham are worth exploring too.

Camden

In this part of town, street art tends to be somewhat more spread out. Search for Buck Street, Miller Street, Hawley Street, Hawley Mews, Castlehaven Road, Stucley Place, and check the back of the Electric Ballroom. Just walking along the High Street will give you an eyeful too. You will find many tributes to Amy Winehouse along the way, as she was a local resident.

TREET ART

CINEMA

Prince Charles Cinema

7 Leicester Place, London WC2, princecharlescinema.com

This is a true gem alongside the huge blockbuster cinemas in Leicester Square. It's the only independent cinema in the West End and offers a great mix of the latest releases, cult, classics and arthouse films, sing-alongs, and movie marathons.

Screen on the Green

83 Upper Street, London N1, everymancinema.com

This cinema was opened in 1913. With its iconic façade, it is one of the UK's oldest cinemas. It's a beautifully old-fashioned, intimate venue. You can order food and snacks from the comfort of your relaxed seat.

BFI

BFI Southbank, London SE1, bfi.org.uk

A list of London's best cinemas is not complete without the British Film Institute. From classics to the latest arthouse releases, the UK's biggest screen at BFI IMAX, film festivals and themed events, there is always something happening at BFI. Under 26s can get discounted tickets for BFI Southbank and BFI Festivals; check the website for details.

Electric Cinema

191 Portobello Road, London W11, electriccinema.co.uk

Electric Cinema in Notting Hill, built in 1910, is a real London institution. After repeatedly closing and reopening throughout the 20th century, it is now run by the Soho House group. The screening room, with its period features, is beyond stunning. With its king-sized sofas and red velvet beds, it offers the ultimate luxury.

↓ ELECTRIC CINEMA

FESTIVALS

Music Festivals

There is an endless list of music festivals in and around London during the summer months. A few good ones, in no particular order, are Field Day, South Facing Festival, Junction 2, Wireless, All Points East, British Summer Time BST, Cross the Tracks, and Mighty Hoopla.

Notting Hill Carnival

nhcarnival.org

Every August Bank Holiday weekend, this colourful celebration showcases the rich cultural heritage of London's Caribbean community. Marvel at the dazzling costumes, embrace the rhythm and sample Caribbean cuisine at this huge street festival.

Camden Fringe Festival

camdenfringe.com

Theatre and comedy lovers, this is your event! Every August, a diverse range of performances are scheduled, showcasing emerging talent as well as established performers.

Totally Thames Festival

thamesfestivaltrust.org

This month-long festival is set against the backdrop of the river Thames in September. You'll find all sorts of activities, from riverside art to river walks, highlighting the cultural and historical significance of the river.

Open House London

openhouse.org.uk

A festival that grants access to hundreds of buildings, landmarks, and hidden gems across the city one September weekend each year. Many of them usually restricted. Great for architecture enthusiasts.

London Film Festival

whatson.bfi.org.uk

Organised annually by the British Film Institute (BFI) since 1953, thousands of film enthusiasts can watch over three hundred films and documentaries from all over the world. The festival is scheduled for the second half of October.

TOURS

Walking tours

freetour.com
strawberrytours.com

Walk the Jubilee Walkway from Borough Market to the London Eye, taking in many of the major sights. Start at the river and follow the signs. Alternatively, a free walking tour is a great way to explore the city and learn about its history, culture, and famous landmarks.

Hop-on hop-off bus tour

bigbustours.com
tfl.gov.uk/bus/route/9

You can take a hop-on hop-off sightseeing bus to see all the major sights. It is quite pricey, though. Especially when you realise that the number 9 and 11 buses both pass many of them, including St Paul's Cathedral, Trafalgar Square, Elizabeth Tower/Big Ben, and the Houses of Parliament.

Boat

thamesclippers.com

Take an Uber Thames Clipper boat. A great route is the one from the London Eye to Greenwich. You see the Houses of Parliament, the Tower of London, and Tower Bridge along the way. In Greenwich you can climb the hill to the Prime Meridian at the Royal Observatory.

Cycling tours

tfl.gov.uk
fattiretours.com
londonbicycle.com

You can grab a Santander bike and follow the Cycle Superhighways. Or book one of the many guided bike tours.

Harry Potter tour

wbstudiotour.co.uk

Visit the Warner Brothers Studio Tour and go behind the scenes of the Harry Potter film sets. Explore the many props and costumes and walk in the footsteps of your favourite character. You need to book well in advance and ticket prices start at £53.50 (but you'll easily spend five hours there).

↓ THAMES CLIPPER

↓ HARRY POTTER TOUR

THINGS TO DO

Barbican Centre

Silk Street, London EC2, barbican.org.uk

Check the programme of the largest multi-arts venue in the UK. From music to dance, film to fashion, and design to photography, there will be something to your liking. The brutalist building itself features in Harry Styles *As It Was* video. Discounts for 14–25-year-olds.

↓ BARBICAN CENTRE

Print Club London

10-28 Millers Avenue, London E8, printclublondon.com

This screen-printing studio and contemporary online gallery hosts weekly screen-printing workshops. From courses for complete beginners to learning advanced specialist techniques, you will certainly come away with some new skills.

IFS Cloud Cable Car

tfl.gov.uk/modes/london-cable-car

Riding 90 meters above the Thames, the IFS Cloud Cable Car takes you from the Royal Docks to Greenwich Peninsula. Or the other way around. You'll have amazing views of the city on the way. The journey takes ten minutes. On a clear day you can see for miles, while at night you can enjoy views of the British capital illuminated against the evening sky.

Smaller theatres

26 Crowndale Road, London NW1, gatetheatre.co.uk
265 Camden High Street, London NW1, etceteratheatrecamden.com

They may not offer the grandeur of the West End theatres, but there are many smaller theatres offering great shows for great prices. The Gate Theatre offers under 30s unsold tickets for £5 on the night. Etcetera Theatre is offering pub theatre. What's not to like?

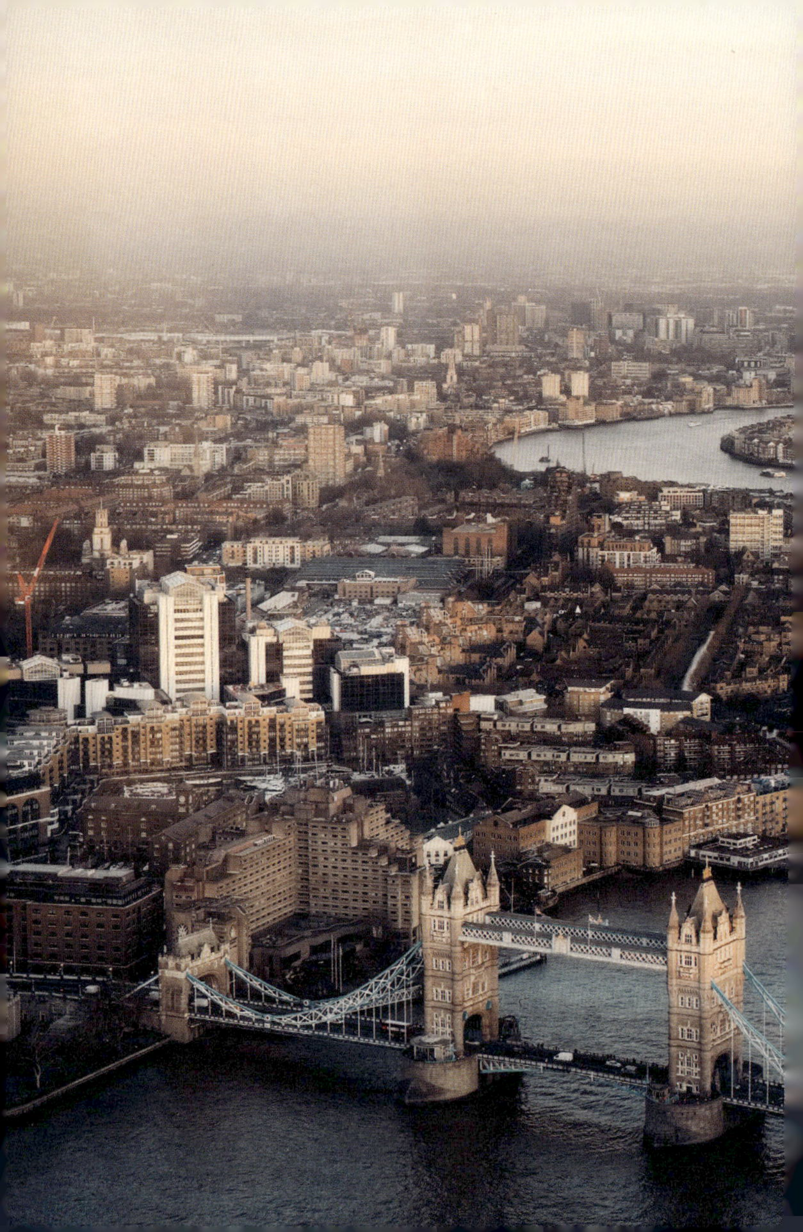

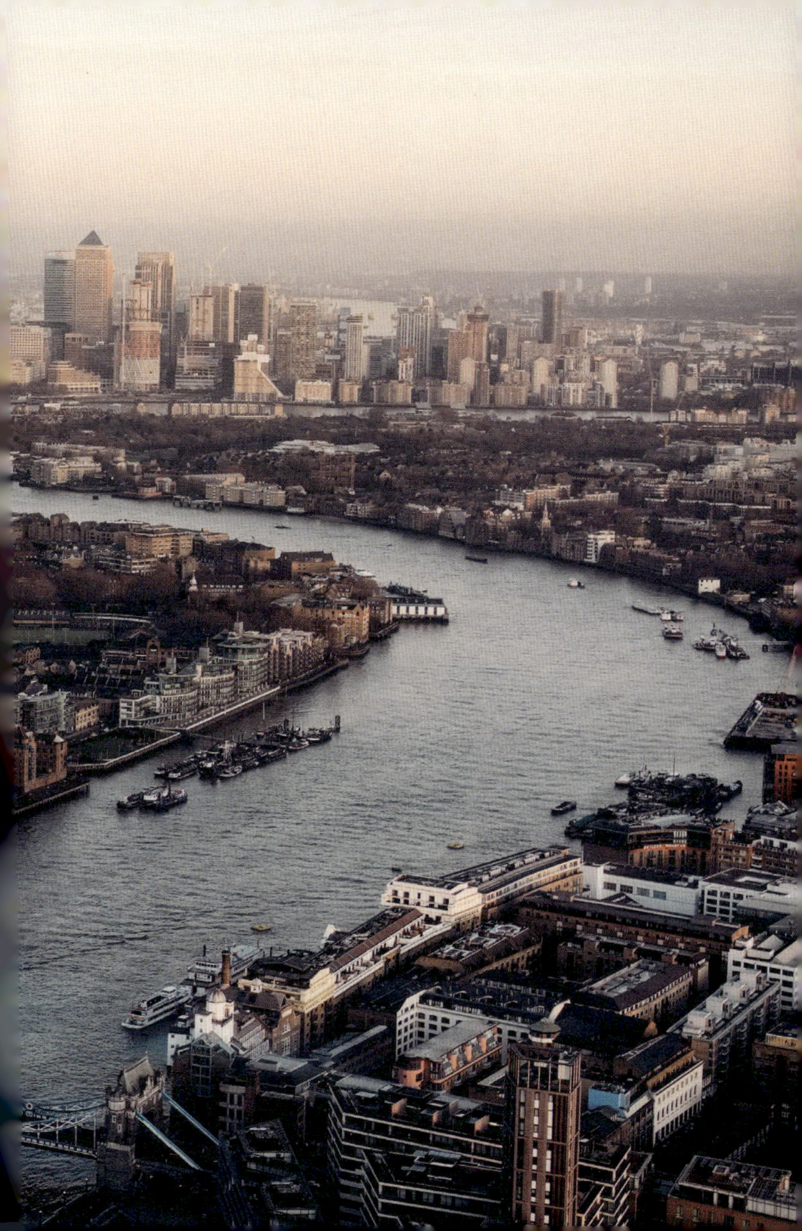

FAMOUS PEOPLE

Adele

Adele was born in North London. She started at the BRIT performing arts school at the age of 14. Six months after graduating, she shot to fame with her album 19. She has since released a string of hits such as *Someone Like You* from the album 21, *Hello* from the album 25 and *Easy on me* from the album 30. She also created the soundtrack to the James Bond film *Skyfall*. Adele is one of the biggest-selling recording artists of our time.

Sir David Attenborough

One of the most iconic voices in television belongs to biologist David Attenborough, who was born in London in 1926. Sir Attenborough is both the face and the voice of phenomenal nature films like *A Life on Our Planet* and *Planet Earth*.

David Beckham

The famed Manchester United midfielder was born and raised in London. He also played for Real Madrid and Paris Saint-Germain. After marrying Spice Girl Victoria 'Posh Spice' Adams, his personal life became more prominent than his football career. The documentary *Beckham* can be seen on Netflix.

David Bowie

David Bowie, born in London's Brixton, is an influential rock musician from the sixties. He rose to fame with hits such as *Space Oddity*, *Fame*, and *Under Pressure*. The singer, songwriter, and actor was best known for his ever changing looks and musical genres. And for his two differently coloured eyes, which was allegedly the result of being hit in the eye during a fight over a girl in high school. He died in 2016.

Central Cee

Rapper Oakley Caesar-Su, known as Central Cee, grew up in West London. His 2020 breakthrough came with his song *Day in the life*. Other hits include *Sprinter* and *Doja*. He is the first UK rapper with one billion streams in a year as well as the first British rapper to gain true mainstream recognition abroad.

Cara Delevingne

The versatile Cara Delevingne grew up in West London. She is a model, actress, and singer. She won Model of the Year at the British Fashion Awards in 2012 and 2014. As an actress, you may know her from her role in the films *Paper Towns* and *Suicide Squad*.

Idris Elba

Idris Elba was born and raised in London. He went to school in Canning Town, where he started acting. You may know him as *Luther*, or Russell 'Stringer' Bell in *The Wire*. He earned critical acclaim for his portrayal of Nelson Mandela in the biographical film *Mandela: Long Walk to Freedom*. Many big and small films have followed since, one of his latest being the role of djinn in *Three Thousand Years of Longing*.

Alfred Hitchcock

East Londoner Alfred Hitchcock directed films for over fifty years, both silent and with sound. He had a very strict upbringing, often a theme in his films. Fear of the police, Catholic symbolism, evil events, and insane mothers characterise his films. *Rear Window* and *Psycho* are two of his most famous.

Sir Mick Jagger

Mick Jagger was born in Kent but came to the capital to study at the London School of Economics. He quit his studies for a career as the lead singer of the Rolling Stones. They went on to become one of the biggest bands of all time, producing songs like *(I Can't Get No) Satisfaction* and *Paint It, Black*. Mick Jagger became synonymous to sex, drugs, and rock-n-roll: the ultimate rock-star.

Kate Moss

The natural look of South London girl Kate Moss was discovered at the age of 14 at JFK airport. Her modelling career immediately took off, and soon she became the face of Calvin Klein. In the 90s she was making headlines for her relationship with Johnny Depp as well as her ad campaigns for the likes of Dior, Burberry, and Chanel. Her iconic style made Kate Moss a muse for many designers.

Dua Lipa

Dua Lipa grew up in North London as the child of Kosovan refugees. She started writing her own songs at 14. *Be the one* was her first big hit. She worked with other artists such as Calvin Harris (*One Kiss*), performed *Cold Heart* with Elton John, and *No Lie* with Sean Paul. Dua Lipa is now one of the most streamed artists worldwide.

Daniel Radcliffe

Born in Fulham, Daniel Radcliffe has gone from timid schoolboy to the world's most famous boy wizard. Daniel started off performing in school productions, while he dreamt of becoming a famous actor. Starring as Harry Potter has certainly made this dream come true!

RAYE

South Londoner RAYE gained fame as a song writer, working with the likes of Beyoncé, Rihanna, David Guetta, and John Legend. In 2024, she wrote history with her own album *My 21st Century Blues* by winning six Brit awards in a single night, smashing the previous record of four Brits (by Adele, Harry Styles, and Blur).

Amy Winehouse

Growing up in a musical family in North London, Amy Winehouse got her first guitar at the age of 13. She started writing poems, that would later become song lyrics. The jazz and soul singer made her debut at the age of 19 with her album *Frank*. She went on to release the world-famous album *Back to Black* in 2006. A few years later, after fighting a long, public battle of drug and alcohol abuse, she died of alcohol poisoning at the age of 27.

Leo Woodall

London boy Leo Woodall was born in Hammersmith. Inspired by Peaky Blinders, he decided to become an actor. He got his first significant role in season 2 of *The White Lotus*. He later played Duke in the action series *Citadel* and the lead role of Dexter Mayhew in Netflix smash *One Day*.

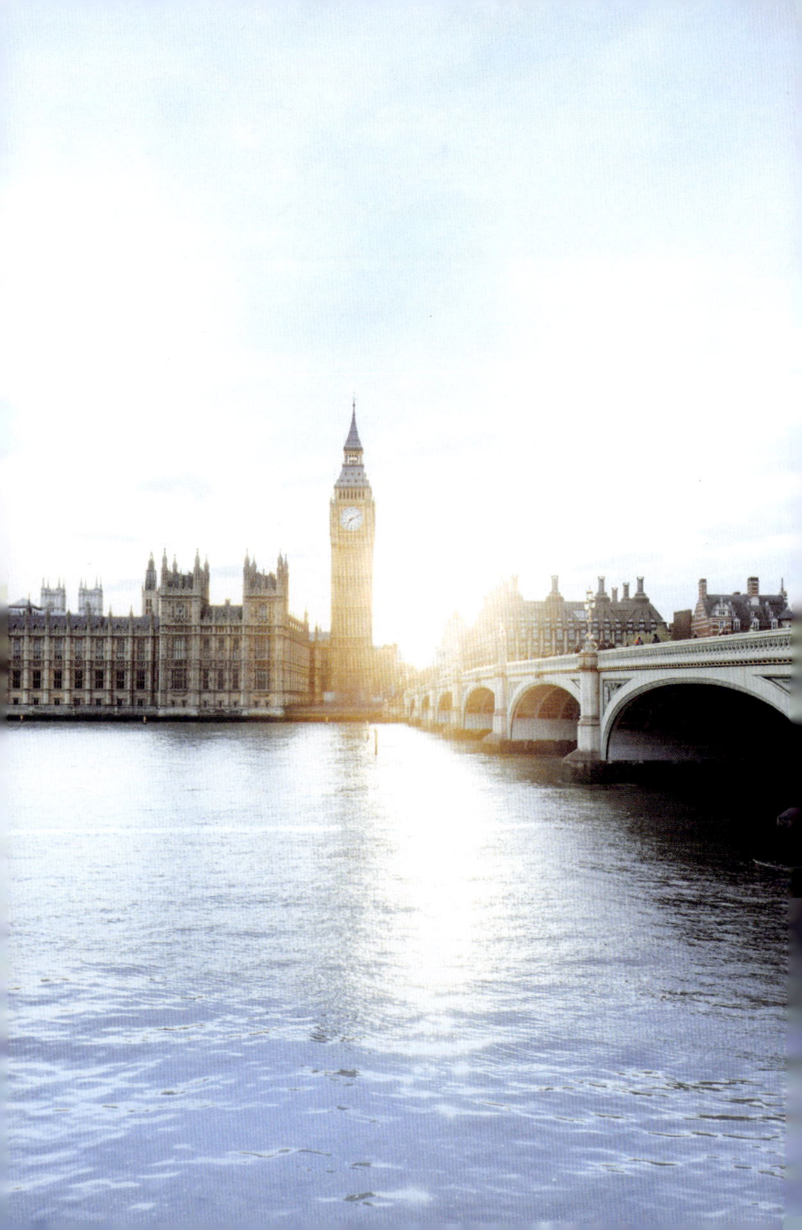

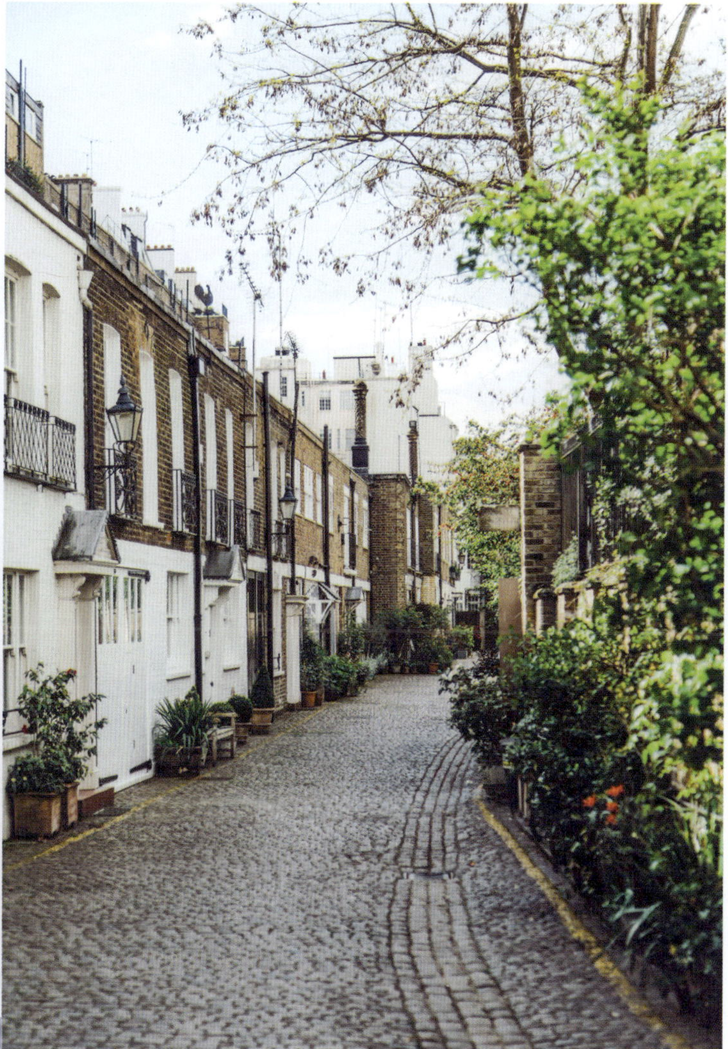

FILMS AND SERIES IN & ABOUT LONDON

London is getting a fair share of screen time. Its gritty side as well as its historical locations speak to the imagination of many film makers. The list is much, much longer, but chances are you have watched at least some of these films and series.

28 days later (2002)

In this post-apocalyptic horror film Oppenheimer's Oscar winner Cillian Murphy plays a bicycle courier. He awakens from a coma to find himself in a broken-down society due to a contagious, aggression-inducing virus. It firmly launched Cillian Murphy's career. The film features many London locations, such as Westminster Bridge, Piccadilly Circus and Oxford Street. To pretend these locations were desolate, they closed off streets for only a few minutes at a time, mostly very early in the morning on Sundays.

About a Boy (2002)

This film might not be the usual romantic comedy you expect from Hugh Grant. It revolves around the touching relationship between Marcus and Will. Twelve-year-old Marcus, who lives with his depressed mother, is faced with bullying. Thirty-eight-year-old slacker Will, living off royalties, pursues single mothers for his selfish needs. Their lives intersect when Marcus infiltrates Will's world, leading to unexpected mutual growth and guidance through life's challenges. Filming locations include West Hill Primary School and Acton Town Hall.

All of us Strangers (2023)

The drama fantasy film starts in a near-empty tower block in London, where Adam meets his mysterious neighbour Harry. The relationship that develops completely changes Adam's life. Things are getting even more complicated with Adam's memories of his hometown. His parents seem to still be alive in the town where he grew up, just as they did when they died thirty years earlier. The nightclub scenes are filmed in Royal Vauxhall Tavern, South London's oldest LGBTQI+ cabaret venue. The apartment block of Adam and Harry is at Insignia Point in East Village.

Bob Marley: One love (2024)

A biographical film about the one and only king of reggae: Bob Marley. The film guides you through the story behind his revolutionary music. It also highlights Marley's fight for social justice, his commitment to spiritual growth, and his message of unity and love. If you've seen the film, you may recognise Battersea Park and Oakley Street.

Bridgerton (from 2020)

Bridgerton is set in 19th-century London. The series revolves around love, gossip, and intrigue in high society. In the first season, you follow the story of Daphne Bridgerton, a young debutante searching for love, as she navigates the complicated world of noble balls and secret romances. Locations in the film include Ranger's House as the home of the Bridgerton family and Hampton Court Palace as the residence of Queen Charlotte.

The Crown (2016-2023)

This drama series takes you on a journey through Queen Elizabeth II's evolution from underrated princess to tough ruler. It tells a biographical story with political and personal events that shaped the queen's style of ruling. Several locations in London have been used for the series, such as Lancaster House as the Queen's home and Waddesdon Manor, which is used to depict the hotel 'The Ritz Paris' in the final season.

Damsel (2024)

In this fantasy film *Stranger Things* star Millie Bobby Brown plays princess Elodie, a young woman who marries prince charming. However, the marriage turns out to be a trap and she is thrown into a cave with a dragon. Is her mind strong enough to survive? The film was shot at Troubadour Meridian Water Studios, a big new facility in North London.

The King's Speech (2010)

King George VI unexpectedly ascends to the throne of the British Empire. He is faced with a challenge: his stuttering hinders his ability to communicate. Queen Elizabeth, the ruler at the time, seeks the help of Australian actor and speech therapist Lionel Logue. This marks the beginning of a special friendship between the two men. Various locations in London serve as sets, including the residence of the Duke and Duchess (33 Portland Place) and the exterior of Lionel's home address (89-96 Iliffe Street).

One Day (2024)

The British miniseries *One Day* is a film adaptation of David Nicholls' novel. It shows the romantic story of Emma and Dexter, but only one day in a year. Every 15th July from 1989 to 2007 you get an insight in their rollercoaster of a relationship. They frequently part ways, only to reunite later. Their encounters mostly take place at their favourite spots in London, including Primrose Hill, King's Cross Station, and several traditional pubs.

Sherlock (2010-2017)

This modern version of detective Sherlock Holmes is set in London in the early 21st century. Benedict Cumberbatch plays Sherlock, still recognisable by his iconic hat. Together with Watson, he solves crimes, murders, and disappearanes, while his enemy Moriarty gets in his way. The series was mainly shot in central London. Trafalgar Square, Westminster Palace, and Buckingham Palace serve as backdrops.

Skyfall (2012)

In the 23rd James Bond film, starring Daniel Craig, 007's loyalty to M is tested when she is confronted with her past. *Skyfall* is one of the most acclaimed James Bond films due to its compelling story and outstanding performances. Most of the scenes were shot in London. You may recognise Westminster Bridge, Whitehall, and the National Gallery.

Wonka (2023)

In a prequel inspired by Roald Dahl's *Charlie and the Chocolate Factory*, Timothée Chalamet plays Willy Wonka. He is the mastermind behind the world's most famous and innovative chocolate creations. He meets new friends along the way who help him transform his dreams into reality. The story was given a modern musical twist. You can recognise St. Paul's Cathedral from the secret entrance to the Chocolate Cartel's base.

Romantic classics by Richard Curtis

Romantic comedy film and Hugh Grant fans, take note! All these classics: *Love Actually*, *Bridget Jones*, *Notting Hill*, *Four Weddings and a Funeral*, as well as *About Time* were shot in London. Mastermind Richard Curtis is the British screenwriter or director of all these films. The blue front door of William Thacker, played by Hugh Grant in *Notting Hill*, became an iconic spot in British cinema.

BOOKS IN & ABOUT LONDON

Boyfriend Material – Alexis Hall

Londoner Luc, the son of a world-famous rock star, is looking for an ordinary boyfriend to improve his negative portrayal in the media. Oliver, a lawyer with a flawless reputation, seems to fit the bill. They make a deal: as long as the press continues to stalk Luc, they will pretend to be in a relationship. But what to do when a fake relationship starts to stir up real feelings?

Capital – John Lanchester

The novel is set in London, prior to and during the 2008 financial crisis. It is set in Pepys Road, a London street a wide range of characters live in: from a dying old woman and her graffiti artist son to a rich banker, and Pakistani shop owners. It tells a story about the anxieties of this era: rising property values, dwindling fortunes, and the looming threat of terrorism.

Confessions of a Shopaholic – Sophie Kinsella

Shopaholic Rebecca cannot pass a shop without buying that one perfect item. She works at *Successful Savings* magazine, even though her own financial situation is a mess. She leads a life of glitz and glamour in London's trendiest neighbourhood. When her debts and the bank's threatening letters become unmanageable, she has to come up with a solution.

The Curious Incident of the Dog in the Night-time – Mark Haddon

Christopher Boone, an autistic boy, has never left his own

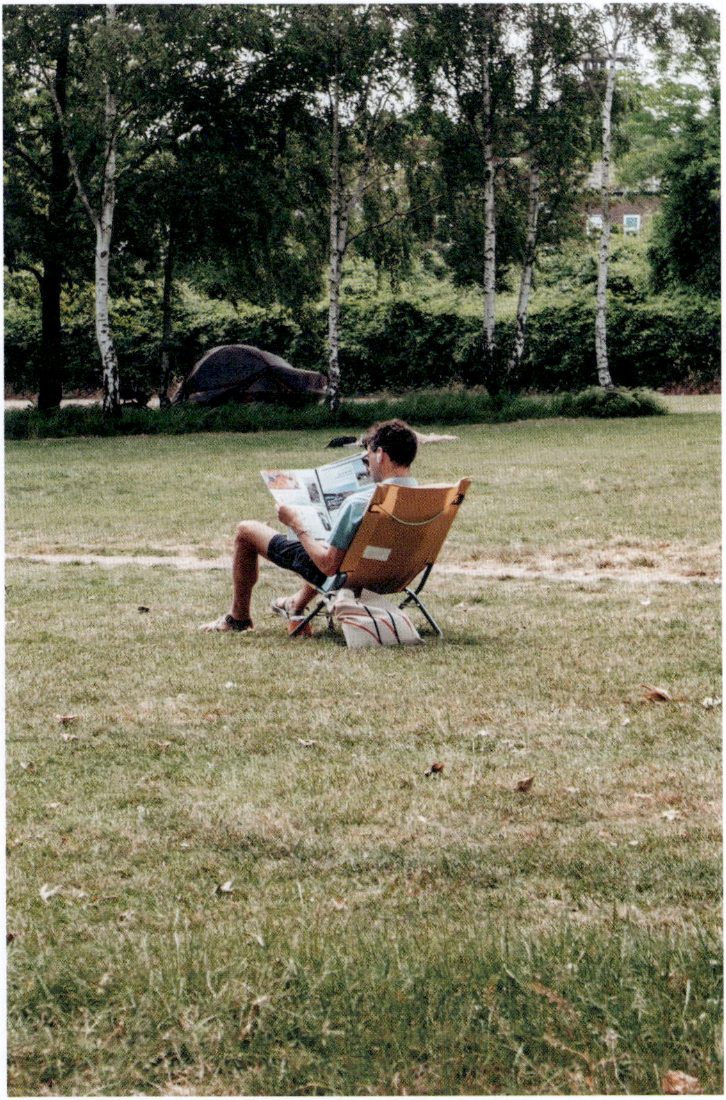

street. He understands maths better than people. When the neighbour's dog is killed, he wants to know what happened. He leaves his street in Swindon and heads to his mother in London. In this compelling story, you'll feel what it's like to see the world through the eyes of an outsider.

Mrs Dalloway – Virginia Woolf

The story takes place on one day in June 1923: a day that starts as a party and ends in drama. You are drawn into the world of Clarissa Dalloway, the elegant and perfect hostess, who going through a midlife crisis. She feels old, her husband is boring, and her daughter no longer needs her. She encounters her former lover and begins to doubt her choices in life. The novel paints a good picture of London after World War I.

The Line of Beauty – Alan Hollinghurst

Twenty-year-old middle-class Nick moves in with his friend Toby in Notting Hill. Toby's father is a highly regarded member of Thatcher's party. Nick becomes part of a world filled with important people, alcohol, and drugs. His life falls apart when the media exposes his sexual orientation. The story is ranked 38th by The Guardian in its list of Best Books of the 21st Century. The realistic description of English life in upper classes as well as the homophobia at the time is praised.

Oliver Twist – Charles Dickens

We look at life in London around 1830 through the eyes of Oliver Twist, an orphaned boy. His mother died after his birth and his father is unknown. He goes from orphanage to poorhouse to eventually end up on the streets of London. He meets pickpocket Jack who draws him into the underworld, and his life goes from bad to worse. Will Oliver's life ever take a positive turn? Dickens' book is a protest against abuse in Victorian society.

Paradise City – Elizabeth Day

Paradise City is about four strangers, all residents of the same city: London. They become connected through their shared history of setbacks in life. The story enables you to experience the importance of a city for those looking for a better life. Other themes in the story are love and death.

Pigeon English – Stephen Relma

Eleven-year-old Harrison Opoku migrates with his mother and sister from Ghana to London. They move into a shoddy apartment, in a neighbourhood where poverty and violence reign. Harri dreams of a life as a detective. When a boy is murdered, he and his friend Dean start their own investigation. The novel describes the search of the two boys while giving you an insight into life in a deprived neighbourhood.

FUN FACTS

10 Downing Street

London's most famous front door, of 10 Downing Street, has no external lock and can only be opened from the inside. Because of that, there is always someone inside waiting to open it.

Forest

London is a very green city. There are almost as many trees as there are residents. So many, by the UN definition London qualifies as a forest.

Sculpture

On Philpot Lane, a side street in the City of London, you can find London's smallest permanent public sculpture, of two mice eating a piece of cheese. When the building was constructed in the 1860s, two of its builders got into a fight over a stolen lunch. One of them fell to his death. Two mice were found eating said lunch. To remember the fateful accident, the sculpture was added to the side of the building when it was completed.

Christmas Tree

Have you seen the colossal Christmas tree that is lighting up Trafalgar Square? Since 1947, Norway has donated one annually as a sign of gratitude for British help during World War II.

Bank of England

Until 1980, all banks in the City of London had to be located within ten-minute walking distance of the Bank of England. This was to assure that its Governor could call an emergency meeting and have everyone attend within half an hour.

Ravens

There are at least six ravens in the Tower of London. Always. Legend has it that the Tower of London will fall if there aren't at least six ravens in residence. To prevent them from flying off, the Ravenmaster clips one of their wings.

Flag

If you want to know whether the King is in when you go to see Buckingham Palace, look

↓ 10 DOWNING STREET

↓ TOWER BRIDGE

↓ KING'S GUARDS

for the flag. When the King is in residence, The Royal Standard (red, yellow, and blue flag with a symbol for each of the kingdom's countries) is flown. If the Union Jack is up, it means he is occupied elsewhere.

Swords

While the Palace of Westminster – better known as the Houses of Parliament – is now home to the government, it is known for respecting traditions stretching back many centuries. In the earliest days, attendees would have brought their swords: you'll still find loops of ribbon in the cloakroom to hang them on.

The London Underground

The London underground, or tube, is the city's most heavily used way to get around. North of the Thames, at least, less than ten percent of tube stations are south of the river. It can get crowded, and you'll be in trouble if you stand on the left side of the escalator. Stand on the right and keep moving on the left. The buttons by the doors serve no purpose; only tourists will press them. The underground is popular with film crews as well: The London Underground Film Office receives two hundred requests to use the underground as a filming location each month.

Cockney Rhyming Slang

Rhyming Slang has been used since the early 19th century, led by East End Londoners. Typically, a word is replaced by a phrase of two or more words, the last rhyming with the original: *telephone* became *dog and bone*. The rhyming word disappeared, and the phone is now being called *dog*. People throughout the country will use expressions without always knowing their origins. *Porkies* are lies and comes from *pork pies*. The word *Hampsteads* can be used for teeth (Hampstead Heath), some say *Auntie Ella* for umbrella, and *up the apples* means upstairs (*apples and pears*). There are even cash points with a Cockney option, which ask you for your *Huckleberry Finn* before giving you *sausage and mash*.

↓ SIR WINSTON CHURCHILL

PHOTO SPOTS

Tower Bridge

This iconic bridge must be in your photos one way or another. The best moment is early in the morning, either taken from a boat, or from the Southbank. Another good spot is the corner of St. Katherine's Dock, behind the *Girl and the Dolphin* fountain. You can also try shooting the bridge from the banks of the river in front of the Tower. But whichever angle you choose, the Tower Bridge is very photogenic and very London.

St. Paul's Cathedral

A classic London shot is the Millennium Bridge seen from Tate Modern, with St. Paul's Cathedral in the background. Or the other way around. St. Paul's Cathedral as seen from the viewing gallery in Tate Modern is also a great shot.

Big Ben

The famous clock tower containing Big Ben has to feature in your London photo album. You can get a good angle from Westminster Bridge. Or even better, head to Great George Street. It is lined with the iconic red telephone boxes, allowing you to get two icons in one shot.

Notting Hill

The pretty streets lined with colourful houses in Notting Hill are just begging to be photographed. Right behind Notting Hill Gate underground station, wander through Hillgate Place, Farm Place, or Uxbridge Street for the best

↓ NOTTING HILL

↓ LEADENHALL MARKET

shots. Or walk along St. Luke Mews, one of the most camera-ready streets in the world, to find the pretty pink home that features in *Love Actually*.

Shoreditch

For urban shots, Shoreditch is unparalleled. It has a unique combination of atmospheric, cobbled backstreets with doors and walls that are used as a canvas for all sorts of street art. The streets around Brick Lane are a photographer's dream, offering endless options for creative shots. Fournier Street is also a great location. The Georgian architecture combined with the colourful street art creates a striking backdrop to your pictures. Just meander the area and you will be spoilt for choice.

St. Dunstan-in-the-East

The ruins of St. Dunstan-in-the-East are very intriguing. This former Church of England parish was largely destroyed in World War II; its ruins are now a public garden. A lot of walls are still standing but there is no ceiling. Vegetation hangs over the walls, resulting in a mesmerising play of light. It is hidden by large buildings between London Bridge and the Tower of London.

Leadenhall Market

Dating from the 14th century, this is one of London's oldest markets. You can find Leadenhall Market in the centre of the City of London's financial district. It is surrounded by skyscrapers and rushing businesspeople wearing suits: a fascinating contrast. The market has been one of the filming locations for *Harry Potter and the Philosopher's Stone*.

Skyline

For unusual skyline shots, head to Frank's Bar on the rooftop of Peckham Levels. It provides fantastic views of the city. Or visit Sky Garden, admire the beautiful views, stroll around, and take amazing photos of the greenery with the skyline just behind. Primrose Hill is another location for breathtaking views of London from above. The iconic hill offers panoramic views of the skyline and is a popular spot for picnics and taking in the sights.

Columbia Road Flower Market

Head to Columbia Road on a Sunday. The flower market is a fantastic place to capture the buzz and the blooms in one shot. The street is lined with colourful houses so you really can't go wrong by going there.

Beatles

You can have a go at reproducing that iconic Beatles album cover walking along the famous Abbey Road zebra crossing in St. John's Wood.

Harry Potter

If you are a Harry Potter fan, you must head to Platform 9¾ at King's Cross Station. The iconic wall with a trolley halfway through it has been recreated making for a perfect photo opportunity. You won't be the only one there, though.

PHOTO SPOTS 99

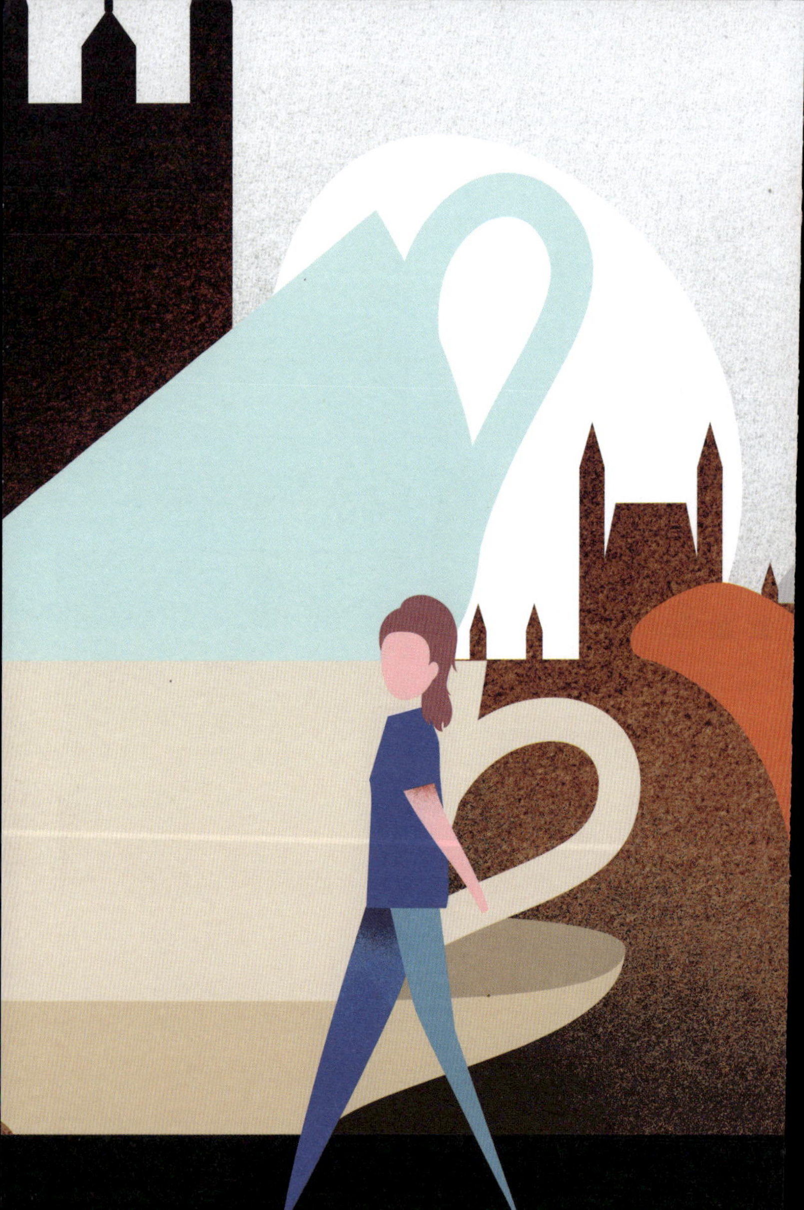

FOOD AND DRINKS

BREAKFAST

The famous full English Breakfast, or *fry-up*, should really be experienced in all its glory in one of the *greasy spoons*, or *caffs*. They stand the test of time, ageing with grace. Students, builders, locals, and tourists rub shoulders, enjoying plates piled high with unfussy food in an unfussy decor.

FOOD AND DRINKS

Beppe's Café

Giuseppe Papini, known as Beppe, started his café in 1932. His granddaughter is now in charge of this old school joint. English breakfast just as they should be, sausage rolls, burgers, and much more. Builders, businesspeople, market traders ... everybody loves Beppe's Café. Closed at weekends.

23w Smithfield, London EC1, insta @beppescafe1932

E. Pellicci

Serving British and Italian staples to the local community since 1900, this little family-run café is an East End institution. It can get a bit busy and chaotic, but that is all part of the experience. Have a *builder's* tea (a cup of very strong tea, with milk) with your breakfast and you will feel like a local. Cash only and closed on Sundays.

332 Bethnal Green Road, London E2, epellicci.co.uk

Terry's

Terry, a former butcher at Smithfield Market, opened this café in 1982. Now his son is in charge, the décor and the menu remained largely the same. Quality is still high, and portions are still generous. The new deli offers tasty takeaways, and they serve an all-day brunch.

158 Great Suffolk Street, London SE1, terryscafe.co.uk

Regency Café

The Regency Café has been serving full English breakfasts and other classics since 1946. On a great location if you want to explore Westminster after. There is always a queue, but it always moves quickly. Budget-friendly, delicious, and comforting – what more could you ask for? Closed on Sundays.

17-19 Regency Street, London SW1, regencycafelondon.com

Mare Street Market

If you fancy something completely different from the traditional café, head to one of London's many street food markets. Mare Street Market will not disappoint. It's not really a market as such, but an old office block that has been transformed into a very desirable East London hangout. Flower shop, vinyl store, tattoo studio, barber shop, antique shop, deli, restaurant, and coffeeshop all rolled into one: it is impossible to pin this place down. You can come any time of day, but it's certainly a fantastic place to have brunch.

117 Mare Street, London E8, marestreetmarket.com

AFTERNOON TEA

The famous afternoon tea has a rich history, dating back to the 1800s. Today, every chintzy hotel serves their own signature afternoon tea. It can be notoriously expensive, and you often have to dress up for the occasion. If money would be of no concern, Sketch offers the funkiest afternoon tea in town (from £55). The Savoy serves the most classic (from £75).

If that is above your pay grade, look out for *cream teas*: just as British (tea and scones) but more affordable. Alternatively, buy some sweet treats at a bakery and create your own alfresco afternoon tea on a picnic blanket in the park. This will certainly save you some pennies.

EL & N

This branch of EL & N serves a more affordable afternoon tea. You can feast on an impressive array of Instagrammable delicacies for £45 for two.

25g Lowndes Street, London SW1, elnlondon.com

Buns from Home

Head to one of the Buns from Home locations for your sweet cravings. Especially their cinnamon buns are amazing.

bunsfromhome.com

Ottolenghi

You could also stock up at one of Ottolenghi's delis dotted throughout the city. Picnics have never tasted this good!

ottolenghi.co.uk

PIE & MASH

London's East End has its own array of unique Cockney food. Many of these dishes were created out of a necessity for cheap ingredients. Cockney classics include minced beef pie, mashed potato, jellied eels, and a parsley sauce known as liquor. It's an acquired taste, but to many, it is the ultimate comfort food.

G. Kelly

This traditional East End *caff* has been serving pie & mash to the street traders of Roman Road market since 1939. They now serve a vegetarian version too, as well as an apple crumble and custard to finish it off. They have late openings whenever West Ham United plays a home game.

526 Roman Road Market, London E3, gkelly.london

FOOD AND DRINKS

M. Manze

Michele Manze and family started selling pie, mash, and eels in 1902. Inside, nothing seems to have changed and some say it is still the best in town. They serve from three locations, the one in Tower Bridge being the oldest.

87 Tower Bridge Road, London SE1, manze.co.uk

W.J. Arment

Arments has been going strong for over a century, passing down authentic family recipes through four generations. They are famed for their stewed and jellied eel, as well as their signature chilli vinegar. You can tuck into vegetarian and fruit pies too.

7 & 9 Westmoreland Road, London SE17, armentspieandmash.com

FISH & CHIPS

Fried fish was introduced and sold by East End Jews in the 17th century, while chips originate from Lancashire and Yorkshire. It is unclear who was the first to make the magical combination, but it certainly took off. There are a few ground rules when it comes to fish & chips. It is traditionally eaten with salt and vinegar and wrapped in newspaper for insulation. The fish must be fresh, the batter crunchy, and the chips fluffy. If you go to a traditional fish 'n chips shop, or *chippy*, you can be sure these rules are honoured.

Poppies

Poppies takes its name from born and bred East-Ender Pat Newland, also known as Pops. At the age of 11, he had a job on Roman Road cutting up The Daily Mirror to wrap fish & chips in. He opened his own

Fish & Chip shop in Spitalfields. Now, you can find Poppies at four locations in central London, so you are never too far away from a decent portion.

6-8 Hanbury Street, London E1, poppiesfishandchips.co.uk

Golden Hind

The Golden Hind has been in the heart of Marylebone since 1914. Its historic charm has gotten a bit lost along the way, but the quality has been preserved. The menu also offers steamed fish and salads.

71-71 Marylebone Lane, London W1, golden-hindrestaurant.com

Sutton & Sons

Classic fish & chips of a very good quality. All three branches of Sutton & Sons also serve vegan alternatives for everything from fish & chips to prawn cocktail, burgers, battered sausages, and pie and mash. The vegan menu is constantly evolving, so there really is something for everyone.

suttonandsons.co.uk

LUNCH & DINNER

On the Bab

This little restaurant serves Korean street food. It is a great lunch spot, but also the perfect start to a night out on the town. Fried chicken, buns, noodles, and kimchi fried rice are their staples. They have more locations, including one in Paris.

305 Old Street, London EC1, onthebab.com

Gloria

This all-day Italian trattoria is covered in plants and florals. It is all about good Italian classics and very good vibes. You will satisfy your appetite while you are set for a fun time too.

54-56 Great Eastern Street, London EC2, bigmammagroup.com/en/trattorias/gloria

Dishoom

The first café, opening in Covent Garden in 2010, was inspired by the Irani cafés that were popular in Mumbai in the

1960s. This, combined with the mesmerising aromas of authentic Mumbai café foods, proved to be a very successful formula. Several locations have opened since. You can come here all day every day. The Big Bombay Breakfast is a good start to your day.

12 Upper St. Martin's Lane, London WC2, dishoom.com

Din Tai Fung

Din Tai Fung is an amazing Taiwanese international brand with restaurants all over the world, including Covent Garden, Centre Point, and Selfridges. Everything is prepared with surgical precision. Try the branch in Covent Garden and you are in for a real treat. The dumplings are phenomenal, and you can see them being prepared on the premises.

5 Henrietta Street, London WC2, dintaifung-uk.com

OKKO

The menu at OKKO on Broadway Market represents the Japanese diaspora in South America and the Pacific. This results in an interesting mix of ramen, sashimi, tacos, margaritas, and sakes. Flavourful and fun at an affordable price.

49 Broadway Market, London E8, okko-uk.com

Padella

Go to Padella for fresh, hand-rolled pasta with delicious sauces and fillings. It tends to get busy, but you can join a virtual queue by scanning the QR code outside. In the meantime, you can have a wander around Borough Market until it's your turn.

6 Southwark Street, London SE1, padella.co

BAO

BAO takes its inspiration from Taiwanese cooking, with bao buns (obviously) being their signature dish. There are several locations, but the original one in Soho remains a firm favourite. Compact, clean, and buzzing, you really can't go wrong here.

53 Lexington Street, London W1, baolondon.com

Kiln

In their tiny restaurant in Soho, Kiln is cooking up a Thai-influenced storm. The best seats are at the counter, where you can watch the chefs prepare your dishes in clay pots and flaming woks on the hot coals.

58 Brewer Street, London W1, kilnsoho.com

Bone Daddies

Come to daddy for Japanese food with a western twist. Everything Bone Daddies serves is homemade and very fresh. The ramen is excellent, but they also serve sushi, steamed buns, katsu curry, and more. They started in Soho in 2012 and opened several new locations since.

31 Peter Street, London W1, bonedaddies.com

Trejos Tacos

Danny Trejo has become a cult figure in Hollywood. He has appeared in iconic films like *Desperado*, *Heat*, and *Machete*, as well as on TV shows like *Breaking Bad* and *Sons of Anarchy*. Together with film producer Ash Shah, he opened his first taqueria in Los Angeles in 2016. Now boasting several locations in the U.S., Trejo's Tacos London is their first across the pond. Expect classic Mexican tacos alongside new inventions and options for all dietary needs.

299-301 Portobello Road, London W10, trejostacos.co.uk

LUNCH & DINNER 111

SUNDAY ROAST

It's believed that the Sunday Roast was introduced during King Henry VII's rule in 1485. It has become a British classic since. On Sundays, pubs and restaurants are packed with friends and families coming for the roast lunch. Included in a traditional English Sunday Roast are roasted meat, potatoes and vegetables, Yorkshire pudding, and lots of gravy. These days, vegetarian options are becoming mainstream too. Many pubs serve a good Sunday Roast. If you want a bit more class, *gastropubs* are your best bet, albeit not your cheapest option.

Hicce Hart'

This gastropub serves expertly executed British classics every day of the week. But it is especially tempting to while away a lazy Sunday here. The roast lunch has several vegetarian options.

58 Penton Street, London N1, hiccehart.co.uk

Cat & Mutton

This place is located on the corner of Broadway Market and London Fields. It is usually packed with local hipsters. Buzzing every day of the week, but they also serve some of the tastiest and more affordable Sunday Roasts.

76 Broadway Market, London E8, catandmutton.com

The Garrison

Informal, buzzing and welcoming, The Garrison is all. The menu changes with the seasons as they have a strong focus on fresh, British produce. It has become sort of a local institution, especially recommended for its Sunday Lunch.

99-101 Bermondsey Street, London SE1, thegarrison.co.uk

FOOD COURTS & FOOD MARKETS

London's dining scene can be tough on your bank account. Luckily, there is a growing number of high-quality food halls and markets. There you can feast on tasty food and quench your thirst without spending as big a fortune. These are only a few fine examples.

Arcade Food Hall

A foodie paradise at the bottom of Centre Point that leaves you spoilt for choice. Several open kitchens offer anything from Japanese to Mexican cuisine. Open daily. A second Arcade was opened at the iconic Battersea Power Station.

103-105 New Oxford Street, London WC1, arcadefoodhall.com

Kerb Seven Dials Market

Covent Garden can get a bit crowded, touristy, and expensive. If you find yourself in the area and hunger strikes, head to this handsome food hall. Wraps, burgers, pizza, tacos, and ice cream are just a few examples of what you can expect to find. It is open daily.

35 Earlham Street, London WC2, sevendialsmarket.com

The Kitchens at Old Spitalfields Market

Take your pick of the vendors selling anything from Indian street food to steamed buns. Find a seat at one of the communal tables and munch away. Quality is high so you can be sure to leave happy. Open daily, and there is plenty of shopping to be done too.

16 Horner Square, London E1, oldspitalfieldsmarket.com/journal/the-kitchens

BOROUGH MARKET

Broadway Market

This is where food-loving hipsters hang out. Street food is only one of the reasons to come. There are loads of shops, restaurants, and cafés too. Open on Saturdays and Sundays.

London Fields, London E8, broadwaymarket.co.uk

Borough Market

Dating back to the 13th century, this is the mother of all London food markets. In this incredibly atmospheric setting, you'll find everything you can dream of. Butchers, bakers, cheesemongers, fruit and veg, and a host of street food stalls selling everything from sandwiches to stews. You better come hungry and make sure you have enough time to eat your way around the globe. It is in full swing from Tuesdays to Sundays.

8 Southwark Street, London SE1, borough-market.org.uk

Flat Iron Square

Squeezed between the road and the railway arches, you will have a hard time deciding what to have first. Pizza, halloumi burger, falafel, or empanadas? You can also grab a freshly brewed beer to wash it all down. The big screen often shows live music or sports.

49 Southwark Street, London SE1, flatironsquare.co.uk

Maltby Street Market & Spa Terminus

Maltby Street Market is quickly gaining popularity with its excellent offering of street food, drinks, and plenty of produce to take home. Open on Saturdays and Sundays. If you're hungry for more, walk further to get to Spa Terminus. There, the wholesale traders open up shop for the general public on Fridays and Saturdays.

Arch 46, Ropewalk, Maltby Street, London SE1, maltbystreetmarket.co.uk
Dockley Road, London SE16, spa-terminus.co.uk

CHINATOWN

London's Chinatown dates back to the early 20th century, when it was based in the East End. It moved to its current location in the 1970s. Today, Gerrard Street is filled with Asian restaurants, swaying lanterns, bilingual street signs, traditional teahouses, Chinese supermarkets, massage parlours, souvenir shops, and Chinese medicine practitioners. You enter through one of four impressive gates, so there is no denying you've arrived at the right spot.

Plum Valley

Plum Valley serves Japanese, Thai, and Chinese fusion in very chic surroundings. Their dim sum is delicious. Even better: gather a group of friends and book one of the karaoke rooms. A fun night out is guaranteed!

20 Gerrard Street, London W1, plumvalley.co.uk

Bun House

How can you not love Bun House? The design is inspired by 1960s Hong Kong, when there was an abundance of teahouses and street food stalls. Steamed bao buns are the star of the menu. Craft beers come from breweries like Moonzen and Young Master. But the main reason to come here is to sample their custard bao.

26-27 Lisle Street, London WC2, bun.house

Mamason's Dirty Ice Cream

If you are craving something sweet, you must take a walk along Newport Court, also known as *Dessert Alley*. Filipino ice cream parlour Mamason's sells a range of very Instagrammable pan-Asian desserts. And they are actually delicious too.

32 Newport Court, London WC2, dirtyicecream.co.uk

↓ CHINATOWN

Bubblewrap

Originating in Hong Kong, these egg waffles caused quite a stir when they first arrived on the scene. Resembling bubble wrap, the waffle is shaped into a cone and filled with all sorts of ice cream and toppings. Cameras at the ready!

24 Wardour Street, London W1, bubblewraplondon.com

Hung's

Late-night favourite Hung's is open until 4am every day. After a big night out, you can come here to tuck into a bowl of noodles before heading home. If you can't make up your blurry mind, the mixed platter is a great option too.

27 Wardour Street, London W1, hungs.has.restaurant

BANGLATOWN

Chicken Tikka Masala has been crowned Great Britain's National Dish. It is supposedly created for British tastes by Bangladeshi or Indian cooks. And London's East End is where to find some of the best. Brick Lane's southern end is the heart of the country's Bangladeshi community, also known as Banglatown.

City Spice

Amongst the overwhelming number of curry houses, it is hard to know where to go. City Spice is always a reliable choice. They also serve an entirely vegan menu.

138 Brick Lane, London E1, cityspice.co

Lahore Kebab House

This one is a bit further out but worth the search. This plain-looking restaurant is an absolute favourite of the locals. They serve amazing Punjabi food, it's best

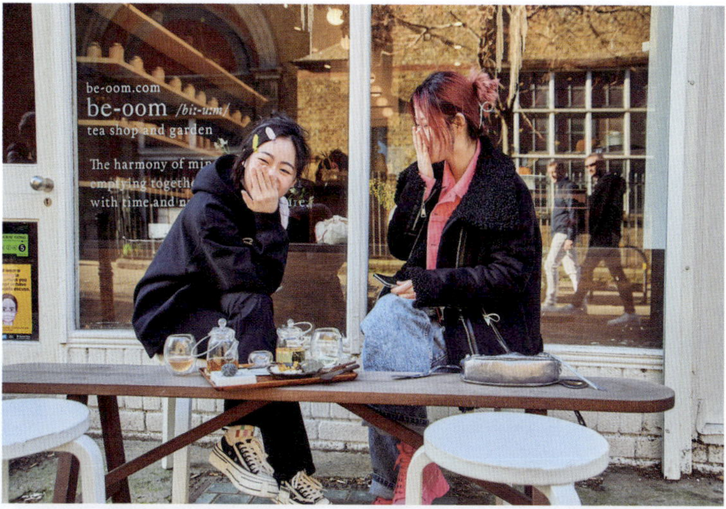
be-oom.com
be-oom /bi:-u:m/
tea shop and garden

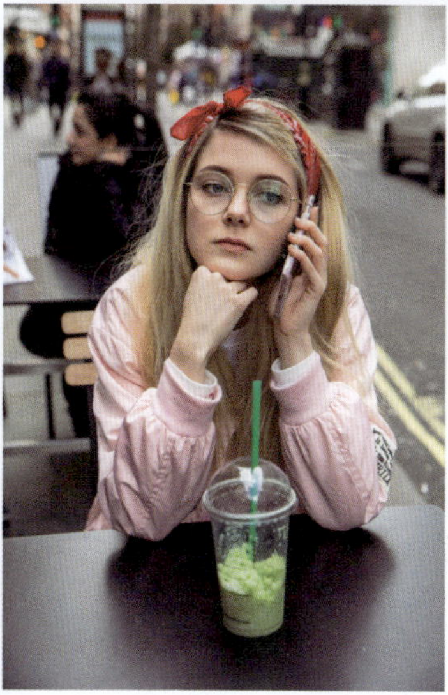

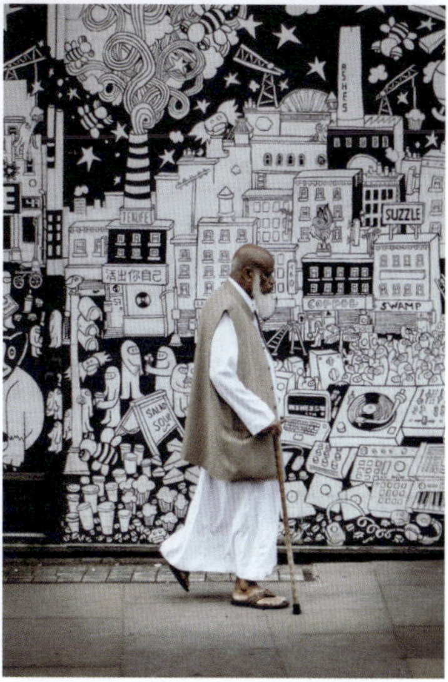
SUZZLE
活出你自己
SWAMP

FOOD AND DRINKS

to share some plates so you can try them all. They have a BYOB policy: bring your own bottle if you want to have booze with your dinner.

2-10 Umberston Street, London E1, lahore-kebabhouse.com

Beigel Bake

You can't go to Brick Lane and not go to Beigel Bake. It is the oldest and best bagel shop in London. They are open 24/7 so there really is no excuse. It is part of the culture.

159 Brick Lane, London E1, bricklanebeigel.co.uk

BRING THE PARENTS

Sessions Arts Club

The food is seasonal and wonderfully delicious, but it's the décor that really puts Sessions Arts Club in a league of its own. This must be London's most beautiful restaurant. Romantic, sexy, atmospheric, and very, very cool.

24 Clerkenwell Green, London EC1, sessionsartsclub.com

Sketch

Sketch is on everyone's bucket list. It is impossible to choose the most impressive part of this 18th century townhouse. Heaven for social media addicts. The Glade is a good choice for breakfast or lunch, or for sipping on a cocktail at night. Afternoon tea or dinner at the Gallery, is a feast for the eyes too. It is an amazing experience, whichever you choose.

9 Conduit Street, London W1, sketch.london

VIEUX CARRE
TENNESSEE
WILLIAMS
BUD
LOVE,
LAND,
COLLATERAL
AND TUMBLE
DRYERS
VIEUX CARRE
TENNESSEE
WILLIAMS
THRILLS, ABDUC
ATTRACTION, LA
AND IT'S ALL SU
COMPOSED BY
SIMON WATERS
JANINE WATERS
DESIGNED BY
KEVIN FREEMAN
CAST
BEN GERRARD
CLAIRE GREENWAY
CRAIG WHITTAKER
KH
OPERA &
THEATRE
12 JUNE – 7 JULY
TICKETS: £10 – £22.
WWW.KINGSHEADTH

ACH
SCRIPTIONS...
VIEUX CARRE
TENNESSEE WILLIAMS
BUD
LOVE, LAND, COLLATERAL AND TUMBLE DRYERS
VIEUX CARRE
TENNESSEE WILLIAMS
THE KING'S HEAD THEATRE
115 UPPER ST
ISLINGTON
N1 1QN
0207 478 01
SALOON
BAR

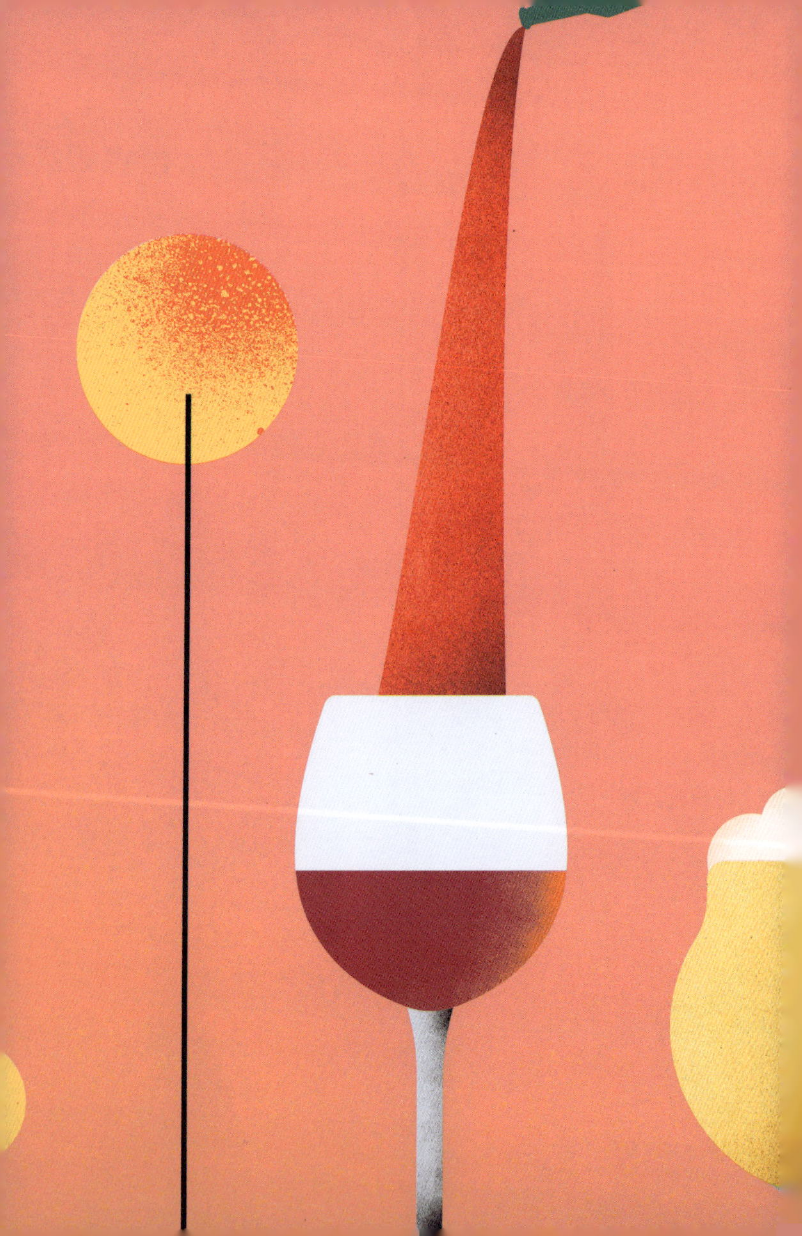

GOING OUT

PUBS AND CLUBS

If you're looking for a great night out on a budget, your best bet is to find the student spots. Keep an eye out for the happy hours most pubs offer. Clubs that local students attend often serve two drinks for the price of one, while offering free or very affordable entry. Check out their Instagram pages to find out about upcoming events, bring your student ID if you have one, and go paint the town red!

PUBS

Pub is short for *public house*, a term dating back to 1859. It is a bar, or tavern if you like, that also serves food. Generally, pub food is traditional, very tasty, and affordable. Pubs often act as gathering places, bringing communities together. You come here to have a pint, enjoy another, and play darts with your friends. If you're lucky, there's a pub quiz going on. Either way, you are never too far away from your nearest pub.

The Harrison Pub

This is the sort of pub we all wish we had locally. Honest, home-made food, including a very good Sunday Roast. Good vibes, good drinks, and some good music to boot. What more do you need?

28 Harrison Street, London WC1, harrisonbar.co.uk

Pride of Spitalfields

A classic, local pub on a cobbled London street. Pride of Spitalfields is as British as they come: a typical East End *boozer*. In an area that is slowly overflowing with hipsters, this good old-fashioned pub is a breath of fresh air to some.

3 Heneage Street, London E1

Prospect of Whitby

London's oldest riverside pub, dating back to 1520. The original flagstone floor is still there, as well as a rare pewter-topped bar. On a sunny day, there simply is no better place to be. Their terrace has the best views over the river Thames.

57 Wapping Wall, London E1, greeneking.co.uk

The People's Park Tavern

It's impossible to walk past on a sunny day. The huge beer garden is filled with benches, beach huts, and a bar. They have their own on-site micro-brewery, so you are in for a treat. Inside you'll find inviting sofas as well as a dining area. They have excellent *pub grub* on offer in case you get hungry.

360 Victoria Park Road, London E9, peoplesparktavern.pub

Royal Inn on the Park

A beautiful mid-Victorian pub overlooking Victoria Park in Hackney. There's a beer garden and good pub food. On weekends, local families come here to enjoy their Sunday lunch.

111 Lauriston Road, London E9, royalinnonthepark.com

↓ THE CHURCHILL ARMS

↓ THE ROYAL OAK

Trafalgar Tavern

Against Greenwich's historical backdrop, the Trafalgar Tavern has a stunning position directly on the river. When the sun is out, it is an absolute pleasure to while away a few hours outside on the terrace. On the menu you'll find all the classic pub foods, including a Sunday Roast, of course.

Park Row, London SE10, trafalgartavern. co.uk

The Cadogan Arms, Chelsea

Dating back to 1838 and recently restored to its former glory, this is by far the prettiest of them all. Best stick to having a drink only, as the food is quite expensive. Or take the parents here for a Sunday Lunch. They will love you for it!

298 King's Road, London SW3, thecadoganarms.london

The Royal Oak

From outside, this looks like a traditional pub. Inside, it turns out to be a modern and cosy affair with the finest in modern British brewing on tap. Five Points, Beavertown, Camden Hells, or Guinness; there will certainly be something to your liking. They serve a mean coffee too, and the food is very good.

74-76 York Street, London W1, theroyaloakmarylebone.co.uk

The Churchill Arms

Dripping in flowers and memorabilia, The Churchill Arms is one of London's most photographed pubs. It was built in 1750 and apparently frequented by Churchill's grandparents. They have some great ales on tap, and they serve authentic Thai dishes.

119 Kensington Church Street, London W8, churchillarmskensington.co.uk

Holly Bush

This centuries-old pub is an extremely cosy spot for a drink after a walk on Hampstead Heath. It gives off a real country village feel, with its traditional and welcoming interior. Classics on the menu include venison and lemon sole. It's not cheap, but it's not the usual pub food either.

22 Holly Mount, London NW3, hollybushhampstead.co.uk

CLUBS

CENTRAL LONDON

Heaven

Soho, the LGBTQI+ heart of London, has plenty of gay bars and clubs. But then there is Heaven, the longest-running gay club in the city. Under the arches of Charing Cross station, you can dance the night away. Free entry for students on Mondays.

Under the arches, Villiers Street, London WC2, g-a-yandheaven.co.uk

The Roxy

Due to their discounts and deals on drinks, The Roxy attracts a young crowd. Come here for a wide variety of music, from hip-hop and R&B, to pop, electro, and garage. Mondays to Thursdays are student nights.

3-5 Rathbone Place, London W1, theroxy.co.uk

NORTH LONDON

Fabric

This club will give you some of London's best electronic music. The legendary London club features three rooms, including one with a bodysonic dance floor, and hosts some of the world's biggest DJs. They often offer student discounts, but it is 19+ only.

77a Charterhouse Street, London EC1, fabriclondon.com

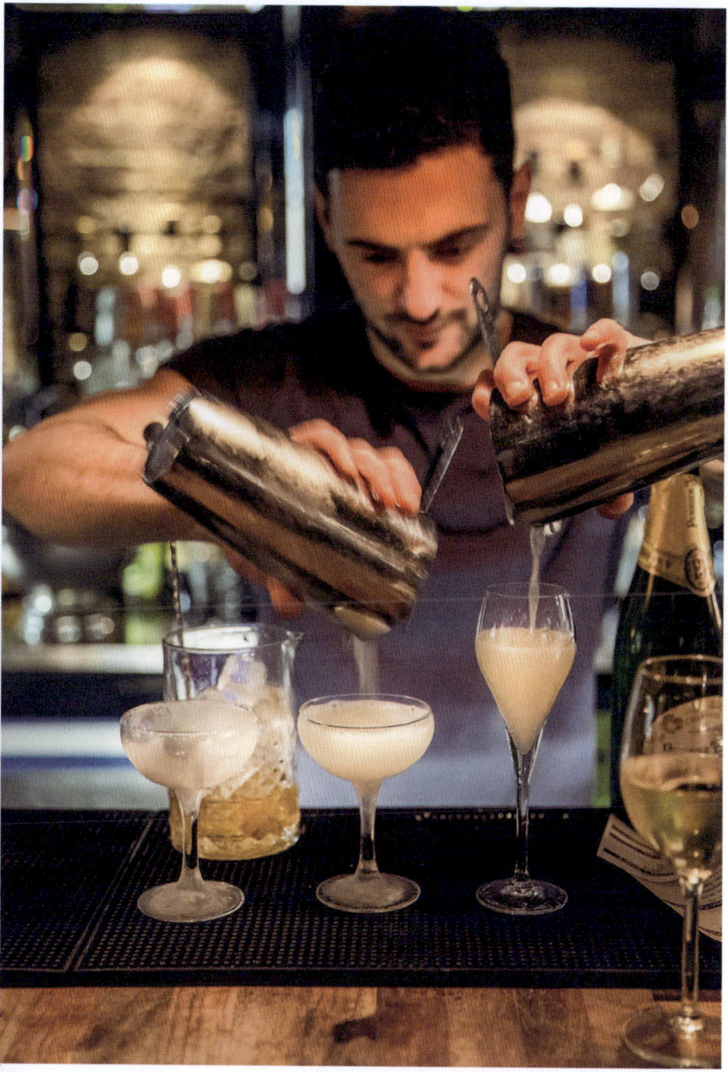

Egg London

In this large warehouse-style club, you can dance to EDM, R&B, techno, and house. There is an outdoor courtyard, a top-notch sound system, and a massive dancefloor. If you want to party like there is no tomorrow, Egg is the place to be.

5-13 Vale Royal, London N7, egglondon.co.uk

KOKO

KOKO London is a live music venue and club in Camden. There's a theatre, there are several bars, and there are balconies overlooking the main stage and dance floor. It is worth checking out the extensive list of upcoming events. There is a very nice café to boot, café KOKO, which is worth the trip alone.

1a Camden High St, London NW1, koko.co.uk

EAST LONDON

Queen of Hoxton

The Queen of Hoxton houses two DJ and live music rooms, as well as a rooftop bar. Non-Stop Pop on Thursdays is excellent for cheesy tunes, while Wildlife on Fridays is good for house, disco, garage, hip-hop, and R&B.

1 Curtain Road, London EC2, queenofhoxton.com

Village Underground

You'll find Village Underground in a renovated warehouse. It is a very cool place for a range of events. Club nights, concerts, exhibitions, live art, theatre: there is always something happening here.

54 Hollywell Lane, EC2, villageunderground.co.uk

XOYO

XOYO hosts three student nights: PLAY on Monday, SNEAK

on Tuesday and Your Mum's House on Thursday. Hip-hop, R&B, house, and techno, everything happens here. Two floors to dance the night away and drinks from £2.50, a night at XOYO might be a good idea.

32-37 Cowper Street, London EC2, xoyo.co.uk

SOUTH LONDON

Ministry of Sound

Ministry of Sound has been going strong for thirty years, starting a record label along the way. It is a very popular club to this day, and it still manages to attract big names.

103 Gaunt St, London SE1, ministryofsound.com

Corsica Studios

Corsica Studios is hidden underneath two railway arches behind Elephant & Castle Shopping Centre. It is an intimate south-east London club that is popular with the artsy student crowd. They have one of London's best sound systems and a non-commercial booking policy: it probably is London's best underground club.

4-5 Elephant Road, London SE17, corsicastudios.com

Electric Brixton

Electric Brixton is housed in an old cinema and offers a mix of live performances and club nights. Not the cheapest option, but their dance and DJ sets are iconic. This is arguably South London's best dance venue.

Town Hall Parade, London SW2, electricbrixton.uk.com

The Prince of Wales

The Prince of Wales (POW) is a pub, a club, and a rooftop bar. House Party Fridays are great for throwbacks and dance classics. With free entry before midnight, you can't go wrong.

467-469 Brixton Road, London SW9, pow-london.com

SHOPPING

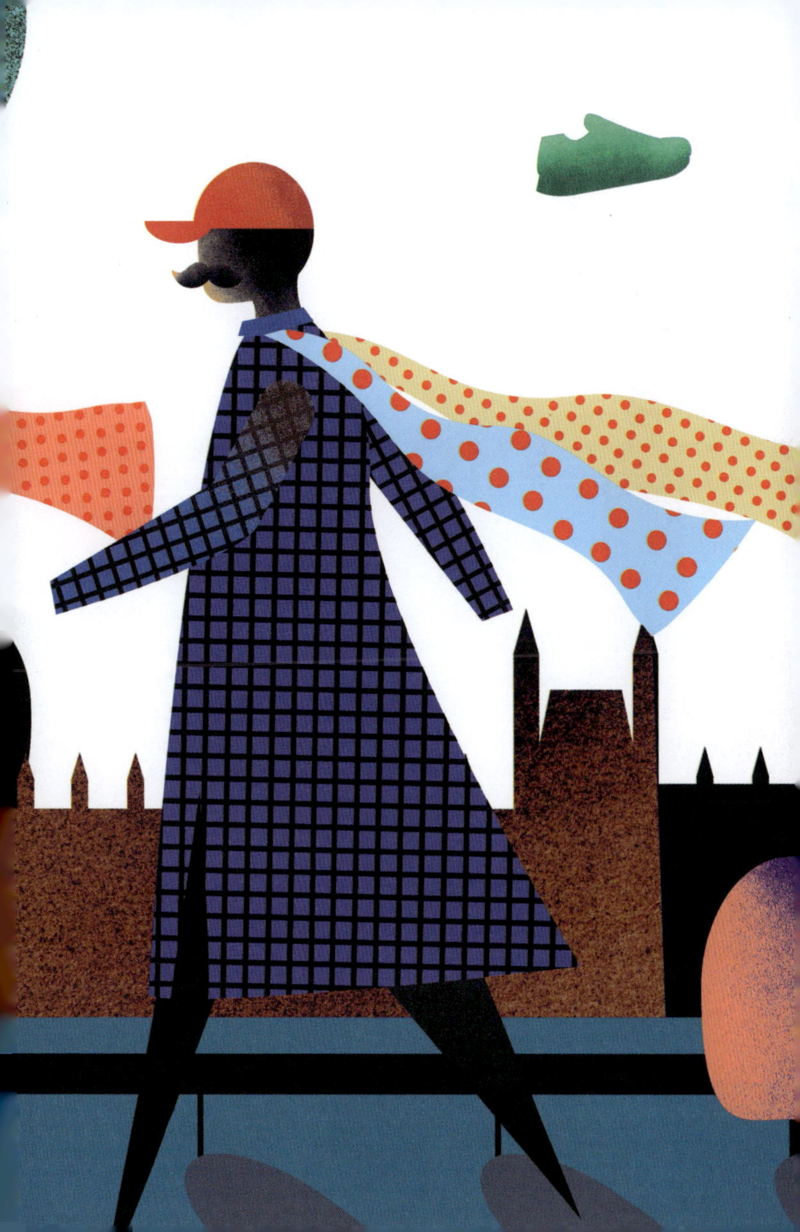

HOW TO DRESS LIKE A LOCAL

'Mrs Brown says that in London everyone is different, and that means anyone can fit in.'
Paddington Bear

London is a melting pot of styles and cultures, which is also apparent in its fashion scene. While each area has its own fashion rules, individualism is key. From classic to punk, and from streetwear to vintage, mixing styles is applauded. Mixing prints even more so. London style is all about expressing yourself, so anything goes!

Whatever the look, accessories play a big role. Statement bags, sunglasses, scarves, and hats are an important part of any outfit. Depending on the area you find yourself in, a stylish trench coat (Notting Hill), a bomber jacket (Camden), a vintage leather vest (Shoreditch), or a structured coat (Kensington & Chelsea) to finish off your outfit makes you blend in with the local London crowd.

When out and about for sightseeing, practicality is key. The distances and the many cobbled streets make stylish trainers or boots your best choice in the footwear department. The changing weather makes layering a necessity. London's notorious rain can often come without warning, so having a hooded jacket is your best defence. Umbrellas are annoying to carry around the whole day, and a nightmare in busy streets anyway.

OW TO DRESS LIKE A LOCAL

VINTAGE, SECOND-HAND SHOPS & FLEA MARKETS

London is absolutely packed with vintage and second-hand shops as well as flea markets. The growing emphasis on cutting down waste, and being more environmentally aware in general, sees new shops and markets opening each year. Rethink, reduce, reuse, and recycle. And why not have some fun along the way? You never know what you'll find, but your new treasure could well be waiting at one of these addresses.

VINTAGE & SECOND-HAND SHOPS

Rokit

42 Shelton Street, London WC2, rokit.co.uk

It started with a stall in Camden Market in 1986, but now Rokit can be found in Camden, Brick Lane, and Covent Garden. They offer an excellent selection of vintage clothes and accessories. Turnover is high, so the supply changes from one day to the next. The flagship store in Covent Garden is a good start. You can also pop into Picknweight in Neil Street while you are there.

VINTAGE, SECOND-HAND SHOPS & FLEA MARKETS

Nordic Poetry

141 Bethnal Green Road, London E2, nordicpoetry.co.uk

Nordic Poetry specialises in rare pieces by luxury labels. You won't find any bargains, but you might get your hands on that one designer piece that makes your outfit shine, and your heart sing.

Vintage Hackney Wick

92 White Post Lane, London E9, vintagehackneywick.com

This warehouse, filled with second-hand finds, is only open on weekends. Here, you'll certainly find that one piece that makes your outfit unique, whether it's vintage tailoring, a cool leather jacket, or a vintage trench coat.

Dukes Cupboard

14 Ingestre Place, London W1, dukescupboard.com

Dukes Cupboard started as a market stall in Soho. They now have a proper shop in London, and they recently opened one in Amsterdam too. The carefully curated selection of vintage streetwear for men has obviously been successful. Expect to find old-school Stüssy, Supreme, Stone Island, and the likes. They also have collaborated with FILA and New Era.

Beyond Retro

19-21 Argyll Street, London W1, beyondretro.com

A London institution known for affordable vintage items. There are shops in Dalston, White City, and Coal Drops Yard, but the one in Argyll Street (just off Oxford Street) is likely your best bet. You'll find two floors of vintage items that tend to keep up with the current trends.

Chillie London

361 Portobello Road, London W10, chillielondon.com

Every single piece is carefully selected, and style and quality are more important than its label. 'Re-love the pre-loved' is their motto. They also have some collaborations, like the collection of upcycled pieces with M.C.Overalls.

Rellik

8 Golborne Road, London W10, relliklondon.co.uk

For high-class vintage fashion, Rellik never disappoints. They have a great selection of timeless clothes and accessories for both men and women, from the 1930s onwards. Expect to find designer labels like Vivienne Westwood and Comme des Garçons. No bargains to be found here, just unique classics. Worth a visit for the smaller items as well as the vintage and flea market at its doorstep on weekends.

FLEA MARKETS

Clerkenwell Vintage Fashion Fair

Royal National Hotel, 38-51 Bedford Way, London WC1, clerkenwellvintage-fashionfair.co.uk

In this beautiful setting, you can take your time browsing the racks filled with quality vintage and designer pieces. If something is not quite your fit, but you love it anyway, there even is an alteration service. The tearoom sells delicious cakes to top the experience off. Check the website for the exact dates.

Camden Passage

1 Camden Passage, London N1, camdenpassageislington.co.uk

The atmospheric, cobbled streets of Camden Passage are filled with beautiful little shops, cafes, and restaurants. At its outdoor markets, everything from vintage clothes to bric-a-brac is sold. Thursdays, Fridays, and Saturdays are best for vintage lovers.

Hackney Flea Market

Abney Hall, 73 a Stoke Newington Church Street, London N16, hackneyfleamarket.com

Hackney Flea Market is usually full of weird and wonderful things. Come with an open mind and you will certainly find something quirky that will make you happy. Vintage homeware, furniture, and paintings, you could easily rummage for hours. Held once a month.

Old Spitalfields

16 Horner Square, London E1, oldspitalfieldsmarket.com

This market is held indoors, making it a perfect stop for those rainy London days. Inside the old Victorian building, you'll find a great selection of stalls selling everything from clothes to homeware. There's also an impressive offer of jewellery, including retro and vintage pieces, as well as stacks of old school vinyl. The street food on offer is of an extremely high quality so don't worry if you arrive hungry. Once you are done browsing, Brick Lane Vintage Market is just around the corner.

Brick Lane Vintage Market

Old Truman Brewery, 83 & 85 Brick Lane, London E1, vintage-market.co.uk

One of five markets at the Truman Brewery. Brick Lane Vintage Market is an amazing daily market where you can find anything vintage from the 1920s to the 1990s. This includes lots of men's clothes, vintage bridal wear, accessories, vinyl, and much more. Upmarket at the Truman Brewery supports small sellers, designers, and makers. Come here for all kinds of gadgets, unique clothes, artisanal produce, and a lot of street food. At Backyard Market, open on weekends, you can find even more quirky and cool goodies. Stalls continue along

Brick Lane leading up to Shoreditch, but you won't find many inspiring pieces on this stretch. It's worth a stroll for the atmosphere and street art, though.

Vinegar Yard

Vinegar Yard,
St Thomas Street,
London SE1

Vinegar Yard is a great hang-out. And it gets even better on weekends, when the flea market is on. Quality tends to be quite high and there are also some young designers selling their goods. Saturdays and Sundays 11am-5pm.

Capital Carboot Sale Pimlico

The Pimlico Academy,
Lupus Street, London SW1,
capitalcarboot.com

The Brits absolutely love a good car boot sale. At these, anyone can sell second-hand goods from the back of their car. This car boot sale is partially indoors, which makes it perfect for rainy days. You never know what you'll find, but the offer is generally quite good, especially for vintage clothes. Every Sunday 11.30am-2.30pm, entry £1.

Battersea Boot

401 Battersea Park
Road, London SW11,
batterseaboot.com

Battersea Boot started in 1999 and is now one of the best organised boot sales in the country. You need to do some digging for the best finds and, of course, some haggling for a good price. Sundays 1.30pm-5pm, entry £1.

Portobello Road Market

Portobello Road, London
W11, visitportobello.com

Notting Hill, with its colourful houses and endless supply of independent shops, bars, and restaurants, is always worth a visit. It can be quite peaceful, but on weekends the famous Portobello Road Market attracts thousands of visitors. This is the world's largest antique market, and it is much more than that. There are over 1,000 stalls, selling everything you can possibly think of. On Fridays, Saturdays, and Sundays you'll find a great vintage clothing market under the canopy of Portobello Green. Their motto is 'You've got to be in the crowd, to stand out from it'. And crowded it is. You can rummage through racks of vintage Carhart, Ralph Lauren, Stüssy, and a whole lot more. There is plenty of street food to keep you fuelled. Continue to the market on Golborne Road for more vintage clothes, accessories, bric-a-brac, homeware, and furniture. On this stretch, you'll find quite a few interior boutiques, and delicious Moroccan and Portuguese eateries, with the iconic brutalist Trellick Tower providing a very cool backdrop.

Camden Market & Buck Street Market

54-56 Camden Lock Place, London NW1, camdenmarket.com

Camden Market is one of the most famous London markets, attracting a young crowd. It is partly covered and very atmospheric. There are hundreds of stalls and shops selling everything from vintage clothes to art, and lots and lots of street food. Weekends can get very crowded, but many shops and stalls are open all week. Buck Street Market is a container market right next to Camden Market. It is the capital's first eco market and well worth a visit once you are there anyway.

VINTAGE, SECOND-HAND SHOPS & FLEA MARKETS

THE H -FI'S
RON SP NCERS
LIMELIGHT RECOR IREBALL X.L.S.
D THE IREBALLS

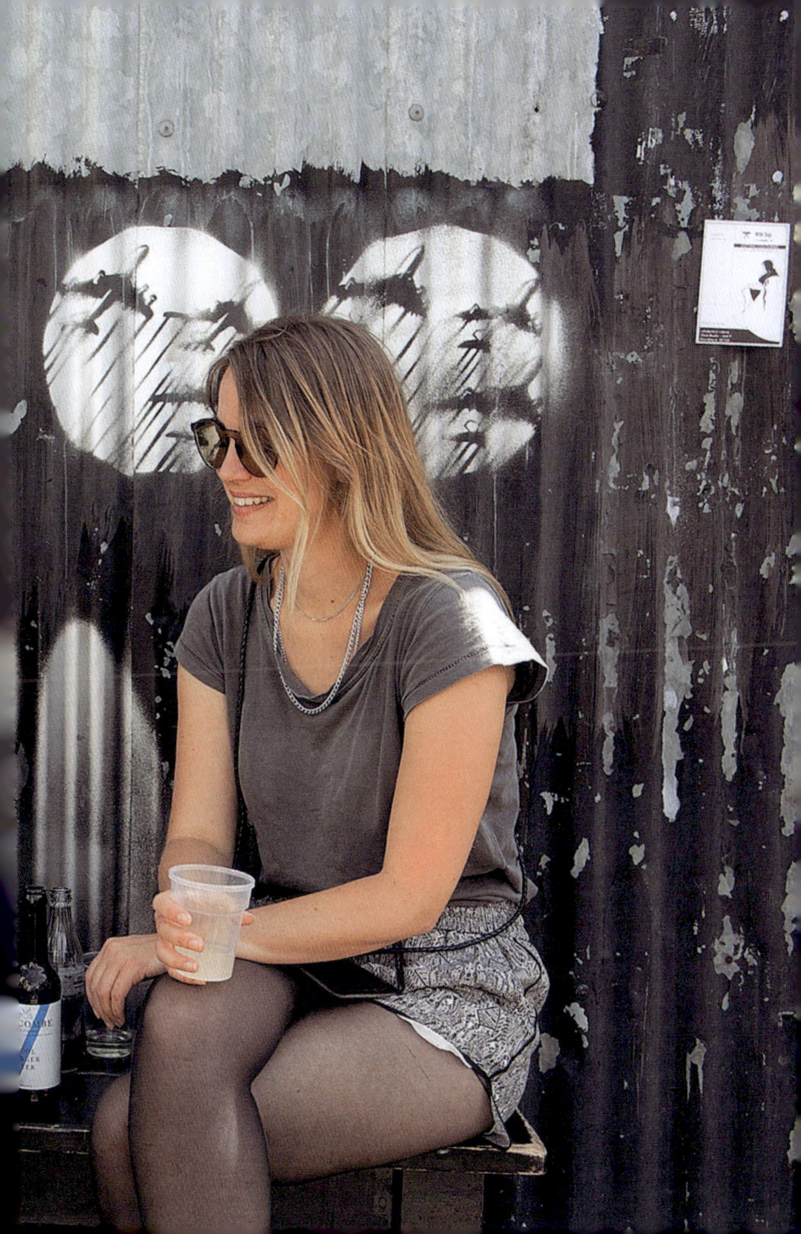

STREETWEAR

Dover Street Market

18-21 Haymarket, London SW1, doverstreetmarket. com

Not really a market, but a small department store showcasing the latest in cutting edge design and streetwear. What started as a one-off, has seen new locations opening all over the world. But nothing beats the original. And while you're there, try the amazing carrot cake at Rose Bakery on the top.

Aries

31 Great Pulteney Street, London W1, ariesarise.com

Soho is the place to be for the latest in streetwear. The beautiful shop of cult streetwear label Aries is a good place to start. It's a concept store showcasing Aries' full collections, as well as carefully curated brand collaborations, pop-up art, and installations. On the top floor you'll find a PaperBoyParis coffee shop.

Footpatrol

80 Berwick Street, London E1, footpatrol.com

London's go to for trainers. Footpatrol is stocked with well-known brands like Nike, Adidas Originals, Puma, and Reebok, including limited editions and rare deadstock. They sell some niche brands too.

END

59 Broadwick Street, London W1, endclothing. com

This shop focuses on luxury fashion, emerging designers, and exclusive sports and streetwear for men. Keep an eye out for London-based brand Places+Faces. It has seen collaborations with brands like Daily Paper, Bstroy, Slawn, and Thug Club.

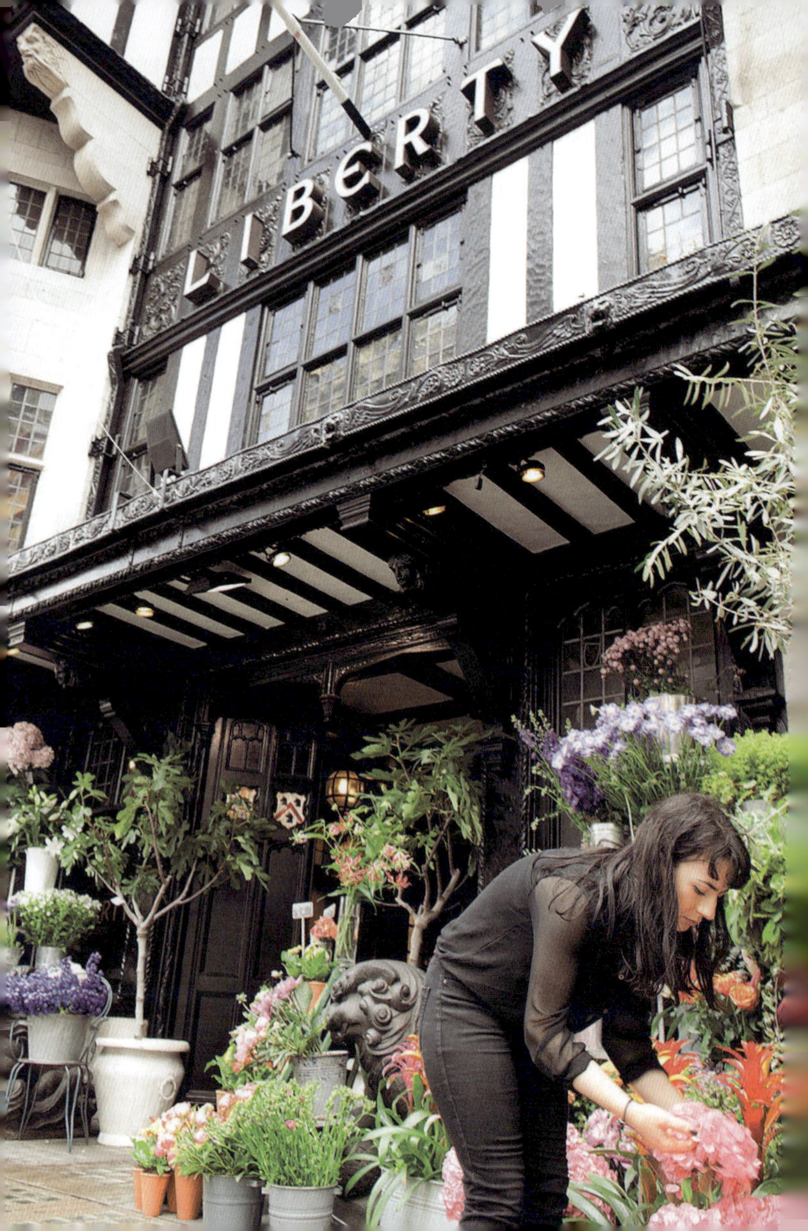
LIBERTY

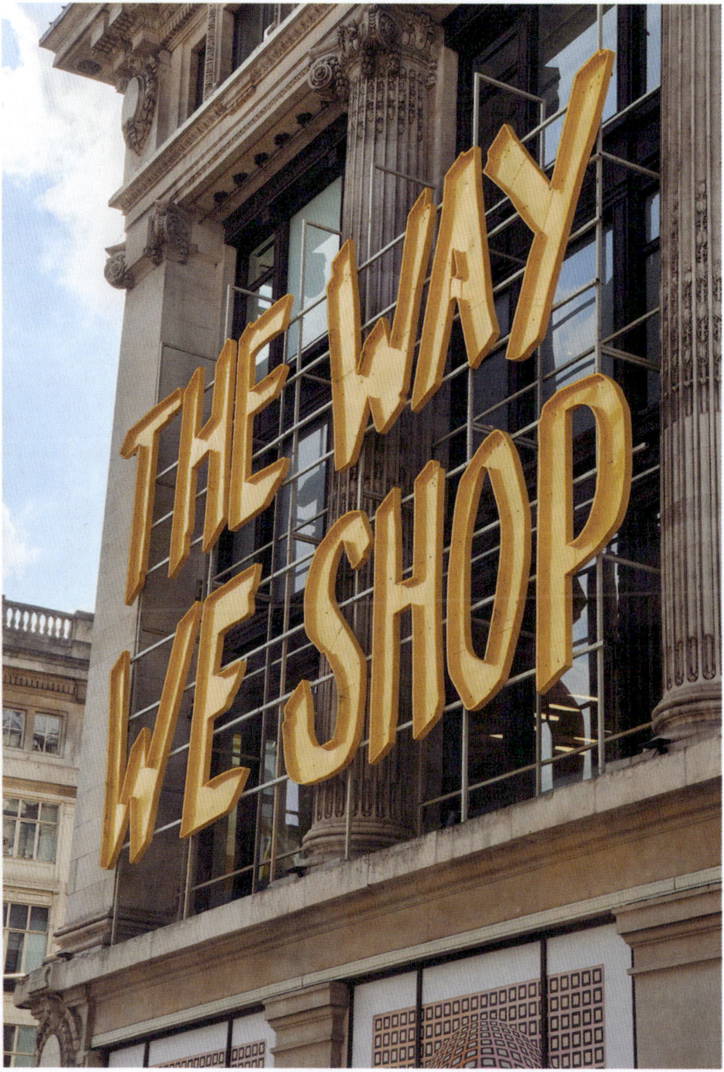
THE WAY
WE SHOP

DEPARTMENT STORES

↓ LIBERTY

↓ SELFRIDGES

↓ FORTNUM & MASON

↓ FORTNUM & MASON

Harrods

87-135 Brompton Road, London SW1, harrods.com

The most famous of them all is a true London icon. At Harrods, you can shop for cosmetics, homeware, fashion, and furniture on the luxury end of the scale. The food department is phenomenal. From August, they pull out all the stops for their Christmas department.

Fortnum & Mason

181 Piccadilly, London W1, fortnumandmason.com

Another British institution, founded in 1707. They sell a wide range of products, but the delicacies are their main draw: this is foodie heaven. And they are beautifully packaged as well. Perfect for stocking up on some edible London souvenirs.

Selfridges

400 Oxford Street, W1, selfridges.com

This is where Londoners go to buy the latest in fashion, streetwear, gadgets, and cosmetics. The food hall is quite incredible too and they have a very good book department.

Liberty

Regent Street, W1, libertylondon.com

The prettiest of them all. Liberty is famous for their prints, loved and used by designers all over the world. They sell a wide range of high-quality goods in their signature prints, but also the latest in fashion, and much more. Go there, even if it's just for the beautiful Tudor building.

Hamleys

188-196 Regent Street, London W1, hamleys.com

Hamleys in Regent Street is the oldest toy shop in the world. Brace yourself for seven floors of fun for children, big and small. They also have three smaller shops, but this is the most impressive.

BOOKSHOPS

Foyles

107 Charing Cross Road, London WC2, foyles.co.uk

Foyles has several branches, but its flagship store really is unsurpassed. It covers five floors, stocking more than 200,000 titles. You can easily lose yourself in here. There's a café and exhibition space where high-profile authors come for readings and talks.

Stanfords

7 Mercer Walk, London WC2, stanfords.co.uk

If travelling the world is your aim, Stanfords is your number one shop. It was opened in Covent Garden in 1853. They have a huge collection of maps, travel guides, and travel fiction. You can also browse a selection of stationery, travel essentials, and an impressive selection of globes.

Booksellers Row, Cecil Court

Cecil Court, London WC2, cecilcourt.co.uk

Cecil Court is such a charmer. The shop fronts have remained the same for over a century. It is filled with second-hand bookshops and antique booksellers stocking rare books and first editions, old stamps, maps, posters, and more. Apparently, this street inspired Harry Potter's Diagon Alley, and that makes sense.

Word on the Water

*Regent's Canal
Towpath, London N1,
wordonthewater.co.uk*

In Regent's Canal, you can find a floating bookshop. Word on the Water stocks a collection of new and used books, with every single nook and cranny being used. Browse the shelves, both inside and out, and you will certainly find a new treasure to take home.

Arthur Probsthain

*41 Great Russell Street,
London W1,
teaandtattle.com*

This family-run bookshop has been going strong since 1903. They have a great selection of old and new books on Asian, African, and Middle Eastern culture, art, literature, religion, and performing arts. Tea and Tattle café serves tea and coffee, as well as a full afternoon tea.

Daunt Books

*83-84 Marylebone High
Street, London W1,
dauntbooks.co.uk*

London's most beautiful bookshop. Situated in an Edwardian building, it has an amazing galleried main room with stained-glass windows. Books are arranged by country rather than subject, resulting in unexpected finds while browsing the shelves.

Gosh!

*1 Berwick Street, London
W1, goshlondon.com*

At Soho's Gosh! you'll find an impressive selection of graphic novels and comic books, from vintage comics to manga, and art books to memoirs. Downstairs, you can browse a very nice collection of prints and posters to dress up your home.

Hatchard's

187 Piccadilly, London W1, hatchards.co.uk

Next to department store Fortnum & Mason, you'll find the UK's oldest bookshop. It opened its doors in 1797. There are five floors, with thousands of books to browse. Although it is now owned by Waterstones, it still feels like entering an independent bookshop. Perhaps it's the three royal warrants that guarantee a royal experience.

Libreria

65 Hanbury Street, London E1, libreria.io

This shop stocks a good selection of design-led books. Its collection is arranged by theme, which means you can browse collections like *Wanderlust*, or *Enchantment for the Disenchanted*. There are a few cosy corners to sit and read for a while.

Donlon Books

75 Broadway Market, London E8, donlonbooks.com

At bustling Broadway Market, Donlon Books sells an impressive collection of art, photography, and counterculture books and magazines, including the rare and hard to find. They are fervent promotors of independent publishing.

Archive Bookstore

83 Bell Street, London NW1, archivebookstore.co.uk

Music lovers should really pay a visit to this independent shop. As well as a selection of second-hand fiction and non-fiction books, you'll find an amazing collection of second-hand sheet music.

↓ DAUNT BOOKS

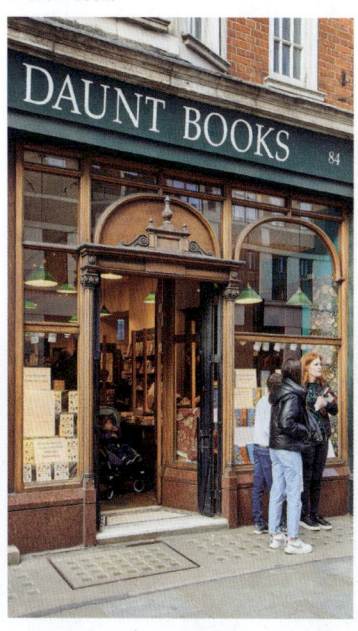

↓ DAUNT BOOKS

BOOKSHOPS

ART SUPPLIES

Present & Correct

12 Bury Place, London WC1, presentandcorrect.com

Named after the saying 'present and correct', used in schools when completing a headcount. This beautiful stationery and office supply shop has just moved into new premises, where you can browse a great selection of vintage as well as new goodies.

Choosing Keeping

21 Tower Street, London WC2, choosingkeeping.com

This selection of stationery is very enticing. Choosing Keeping wishes for their customers to be considerate in their choices, and to enjoy their purchases for years to come, hence the name.

London Graphic Centre

16-18 Shelton Street, London WC2, londongraphics.co.uk

The go-to place for artists of all kinds for over fifty years. Paper, paint, clay, or stationery – your creative self will jump for joy in here. You'll find big brands as well as names you never heard of and they offer thoughtful advice.

Atlantis

Unit 1, Bayford Street Industrial Centre, London E8, atlantisart.co.uk

From beginner to professional: a must for art supplies. Atlantis has been supplying East End creatives for nearly fifty years; from canvas to pastels, and from clay to glue, you will find it here.

McCulloch & Wallis

25-26 Poland Street, London W1, macculloch-wallis.co.uk

McCulloch & Wallis stock fabrics on the ground floor, and an impressive selection of haberdashery in the basement. Renowned for their large range of trimmings, and all sorts of millinery supplies, sewing equipment, threads, and more.

AFFORDABLE ART AND HOME DECO

Backyard Market

The Old Truman Brewery, 146 Brick Lane, London E1, backyardmarket.co.uk

This arts and crafts market can be found in the Old Truman Brewery. Here you'll find prints, mosaics, ceramics, and many more goodies to decorate your home.

Columbia Road

Columbia Road, London E2, columbiaroad.info

The street that is mainly known for its Sunday flower market is home to some pretty nice homeware shops. Some are open during the week as well. Try Nelly Duff for prints, Milagros for artisan Mexican homeware, Straw for vintage baskets, Nom for ceramics, and the vintage shops for all-sorts.

Print Club London

Unit 3, 10-28 Millers Avenue, London E8, printclublondon.com

A good spot to buy or make art. Print Club London is a screen-printing studio as well as a contemporary gallery. The gallery is open by appointment.

Royal Academy of Arts Summer Exhibition

Burlington House, Piccadilly, London W1, royalacademy.org.uk

RA's renowned Summer Exhibition features new and recent art created by everyone, from emerging artists to the biggest names in contemporary art. For more than 250 years it has been showcasing a variety of work in all media. It's a great place to pick up some art.

↓ COLUMBIA ROAD

AFFORDABLE ART AND HOME DECO

RECORD SHOPS

Reckless Records

30 Berwick Street, London W1, reckless.co.uk

Everything from rock to reggae, it is well worth your time to have a rummage through the crates of records in this Soho shop. Look closely, and you'll see the shopfront on the album cover of Oasis's *(What's the Story) Morning Glory*.

Third Man Records

1 Marshall Street, London W1, thirdmanrecords.com

Owned by rockstar Jack White, Third Man Records offers two floors of vinyl, music merch, and wonderful gear. There is an intimate live music venue in the basement and a recording booth to get your music straight to vinyl.

Rough Trade East

Old Truman Brewery, 91 Brick Lane, London E1, roughtrade.com

Rough Trade, the famous music label, is also an independent record store. They stock a wide range of vinyl and merchandise and regularly host in-store performances by up-and-coming musicians.

World of Echo

128 Columbia Road, London E2, worldofechomusic.com

Hidden behind the blooms of Columbia Road flower market, this excellent little record shop specialises in rare and one-off releases, from experimental sessions by unknown artists to weird and wonderful oddities by legendary bands. And plenty of commercial releases too.

Sounds that Swing

88 Parkway, London NW1, nohitrecords.co.uk

Sounds That Swing specialises in rockabilly and blues records. There's quite a good collection of female-fronted soul and R&B too.

SHOPS WE LOVE

House of MinaLima

157 Wardour Street, London E1, minalima.com

If you're a fan of Harry Potter, you must make a trip to House of MinaLima. This gallery and shop is owned by Miraphora Mina and Eduardo Lima, the graphic design duo who worked on the Harry Potter and the Fantastic Beasts films. You can discover original props from the films in the gallery section and explore some amazing memorabilia in the shop.

Gods Own Junkyard

Unit 12 Ravenswood Ind Estate, Shernhall Street, London E17, godsownjunkyard.co.uk

It is quite a trek, but this neon sign nirvana is worth it. God's Own Junkyard showcases the late artist Chris Bracey's personal collection, including his signage for Soho sex clubs in the 60s and his work for the film industry, like the pieces that were used in *Captain America* and *Eyes Wide Shut*. It is housed in an industrial area with several local brewers and street food stalls dotted around, but there is also an excellent café in the Junkyard itself.

Lock & Co Hatters

6 St. James's Street, London SW1, lockhatters.com

If you are partial to hats and caps, this is your shop. Established in 1676, Lock & Co is the oldest hat shop in the world. They invented the original bowler hat, and their hats are loved by royals and celebrities alike.

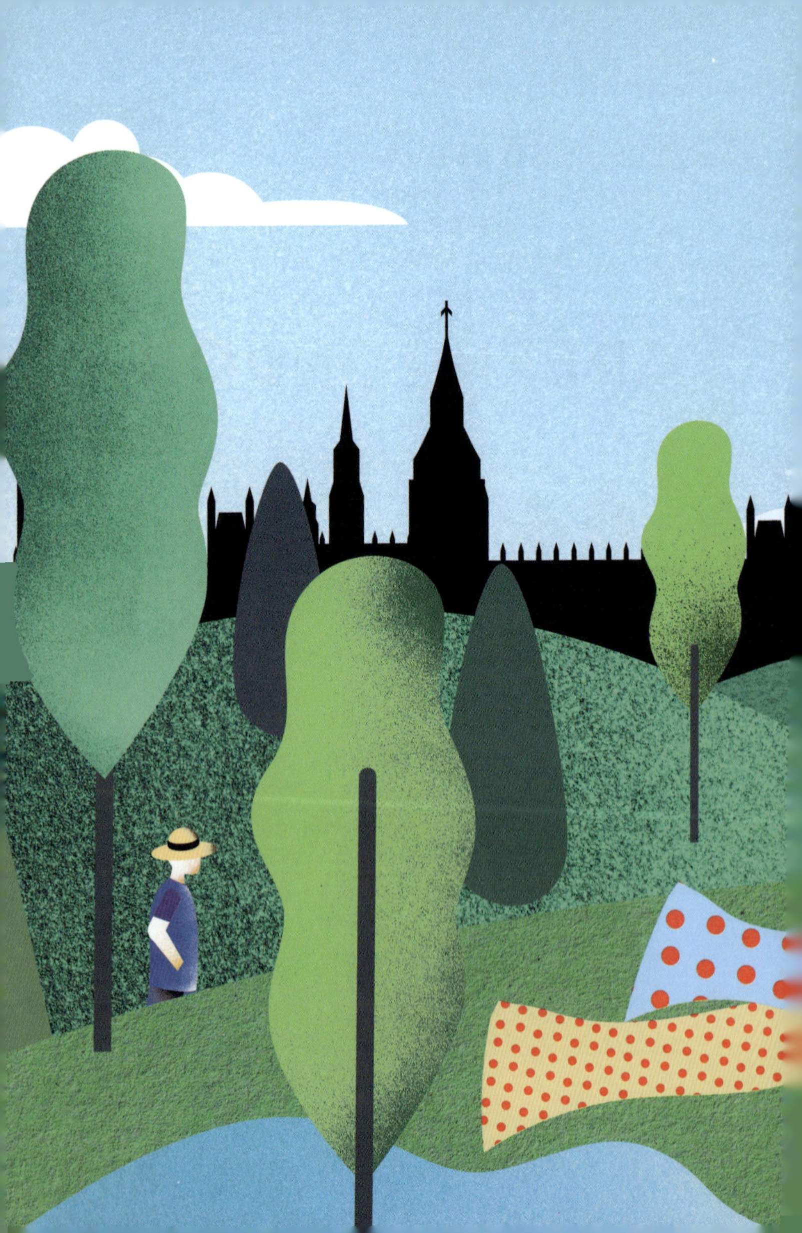

GREEN LONDON

PARKS AND SWIMMING

Let's go to the park. There are literally hundreds of parks, each with their own personality and landscape. Since you will stumble upon some without even trying, here are some suggestions beyond the obvious.

London Fields

London Fields West Side, London E8, better.org.uk

A great park to hang out with the locals, mainly hipster East Londoners. There are two tennis courts that anyone can use. But if you want to cool off instead, head to the Lido. London Fields Lido is a 50m heated outdoor swimming pool that's open year-round. There's also a café, a large sundeck, and a sunbathing area that generally expands during the summer months. There are plenty of nice bars and restaurants around the fringes of the park too.

Greenwich Park

Greenwich, London SE10,
royalparks.org.uk

It is magical to walk around the Maritime Greenwich UNESCO World Heritage Site along the banks of the River Thames. Greenwich Park is the oldest enclosed Royal Park and covers 74 hectares. There has been a settlement at this spot since Roman times. There are rose and herb gardens, a children's playground, walkways, and lots of squirrels. And then there is the magnificent Old Royal Naval College, the Maritime Museum, and Queen's House. Climb the hill, and you'll be rewarded with an amazing view beyond the historic buildings, across the river, to the shining skyscrapers of Canary Wharf. On the hill you'll find the Royal Observatory, home of Greenwich Mean Time (GMT) and the Prime Meridian.

Hyde Park

Hyde Park, London W2,
royalparks.org.uk

As Hyde Park is right in the middle of central London, you will find yourself in it sooner or later. It offers extensive green spaces, a rose garden, and lakes. But not everyone knows that a part of the Serpentine is cordoned off for swimming. Wild swimming in the Serpentine is an amazing experience. Serpentine Lido is open throughout the summer months. The adjoining café is a beautiful spot to enjoy some refreshments.

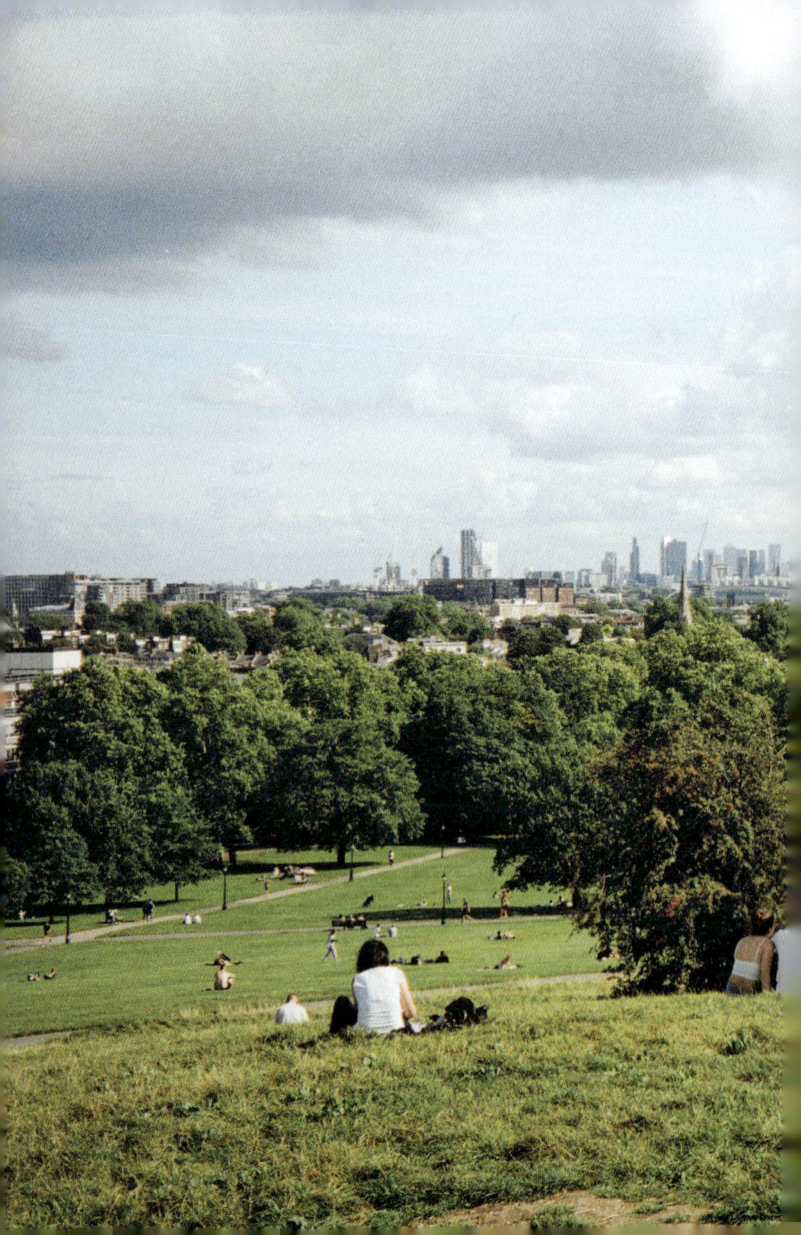

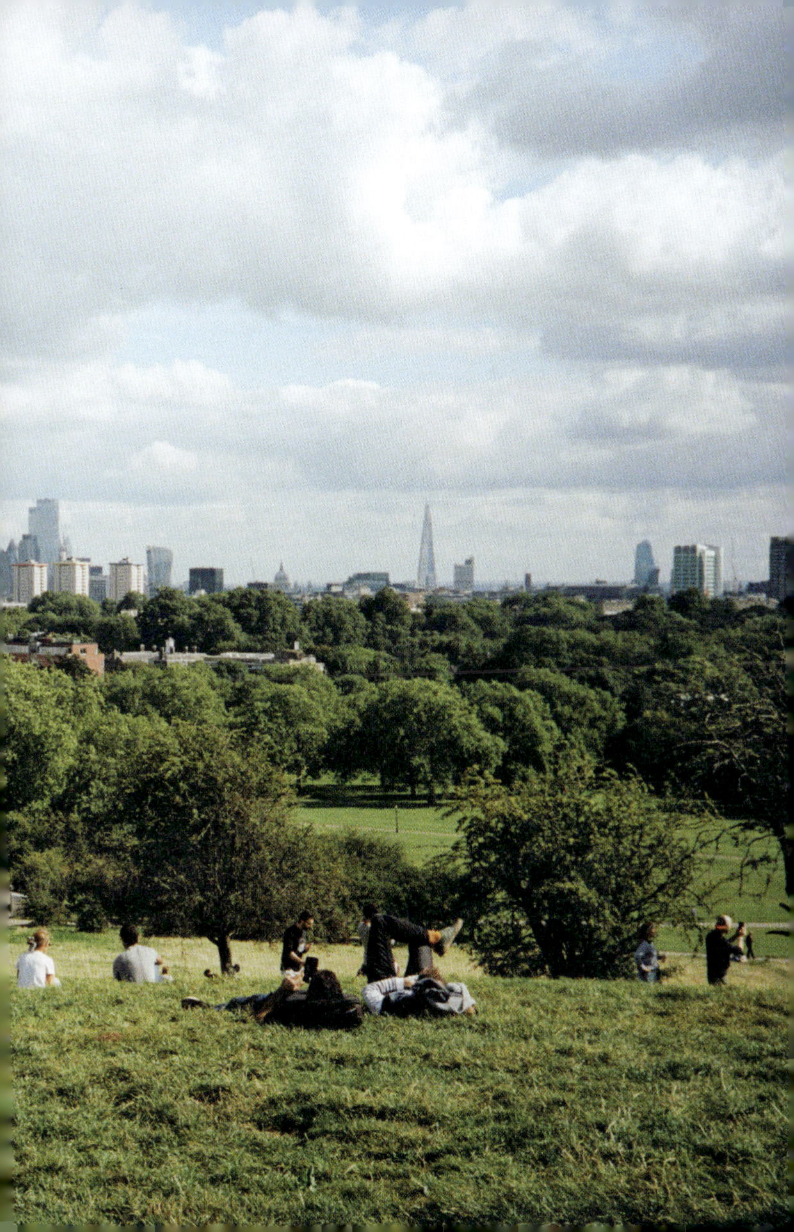

Hampstead Heath

Hampstead Heath, London NW3, hampsteadheath.net

Spanning 320 hectares, you need to plan your visit to Hampstead Heath. You will find a small zoo, a butterfly house, pergolas, walking paths, tennis courts, all-weather table tennis tables, and much more. You can visit Kenwood House or head to the top of Parliament Hill for an amazing view of London's skyline. If you want to take a dip, look for the ponds. Highgate Men's Pond, Kenwood Ladies' Pond, and Hampstead Mixed Pond are open year-round. All three are fed by the springs of the Fleet River and the water is cold! Alternatively, head to Parliament Hill Lido, dating back to 1939. This historic outdoor pool offers an amazing setting for your morning dip.

Kew Royal Botanic Gardens

Kew, Richmond, TW9, kew.org

Kew Gardens are worth a visit any time of year. It has the greatest glasshouse in the world, which is spectacular. Outside, you can easily spend an entire day enjoying its abundant greenery. In spring, the Gardens transform into something out of a fairy tale. Take a stroll down Cherry Walk during April's cherry blossom season. Wander through bluebell woods, accompanied by loads of happy bees and butterflies, and enjoy a picnic among the daffodils. Heaven.

Richmond Park & Petersham Nurseries

Richmond, TW10, www.royalparks.org.uk Church Lane, Off Petersham Road, Richmond TW10, petershamnurseries.com

Richmond Park is designated as a conservation area. If the crowds and concrete are getting to you, this is where you need to go. It's a staggering 955 hectares of open grasslands, woodland trails, flower gardens, and home to a few hundred deer. Petersham Nurseries is the perfect spot to relax once you're done. If you think garden centres can't be cool, think again. You will want to live here. Just enjoy a cup of tea in the teahouse or blow the budget at the restaurant. Either way, it is worth the trip to soak up the typically British atmosphere alone.

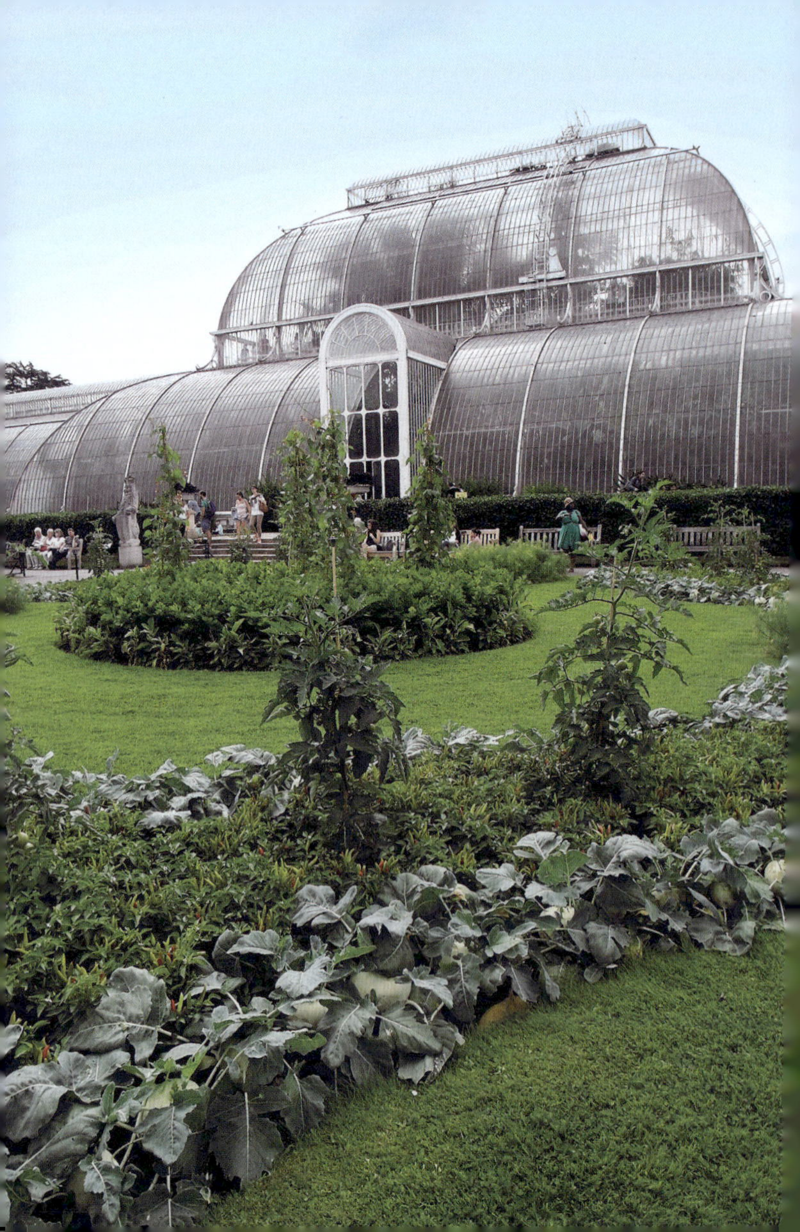

↓ KEW ROYAL BOTANIC GARDENS

VEGETARIAN AND VEGAN LONDON

London is paradise for both vegans and vegetarians. You are spoilt for choice anyway, as most restaurants offer exciting and creative veggie options. Here are a few highly recommendable cafes and restaurants serving nothing but plant-based goodness. Make sure to book in advance if you really want to go somewhere.

Mildreds

Mildreds has been a forerunner in vegetarian cooking since 1988. With five branches to its name, now serving a fully vegan menu, it is obviously still going strong. For very good reason. Fuss-free, welcoming, and offering reliable and affordable quality, you really can't go wrong here.

mildreds.com

Sagar

Looking for affordable, tasty vegetarian South Indian food? Then Sagar fits the bill perfectly. All five locations serve a wide variety of vegan dishes too. There really is too much to choose from, but the *dosa*, pancakes stuffed with veggies, are certainly delicious.

sagarrestaurant.co.uk

Jam Delish

A vegan Caribbean restaurant and cocktail bar, doesn't that sound like a brilliant combination? You go to Jam Delish for Caribbean classics like curries, stews, and wings that have been veganised in a surprising manner. Every bite is full of flavour and their cocktails are spot-on too.

1 Tolpuddle St, London N1, jamdelish.co.uk

Tofu Vegan

This excellent vegan Chinese restaurant is about so much more than tofu. Dongbei sweet potato noodles, stir-fried lotus root, deep-fried asparagus, dim sum, Chongqing-style 'chicken', Xinjiang-style 'lamb': the entire menu is absolute heaven for vegan diners. There are three locations, but the one in Spitalfields is the nicest.

54 Commercial Street, London E1, tofuvegan.com

Bubala

With a vegetarian menu full of ingredients and flavours from the cuisines of the Middle East, Israel, and the Mediterranean, Bubala has quickly established a name for itself. It all started in Spitalfields and now they have a branch in Soho too. If you have something to celebrate, Bubala should be on your list.

65 Commercial Street, London E1, bubala.co.uk

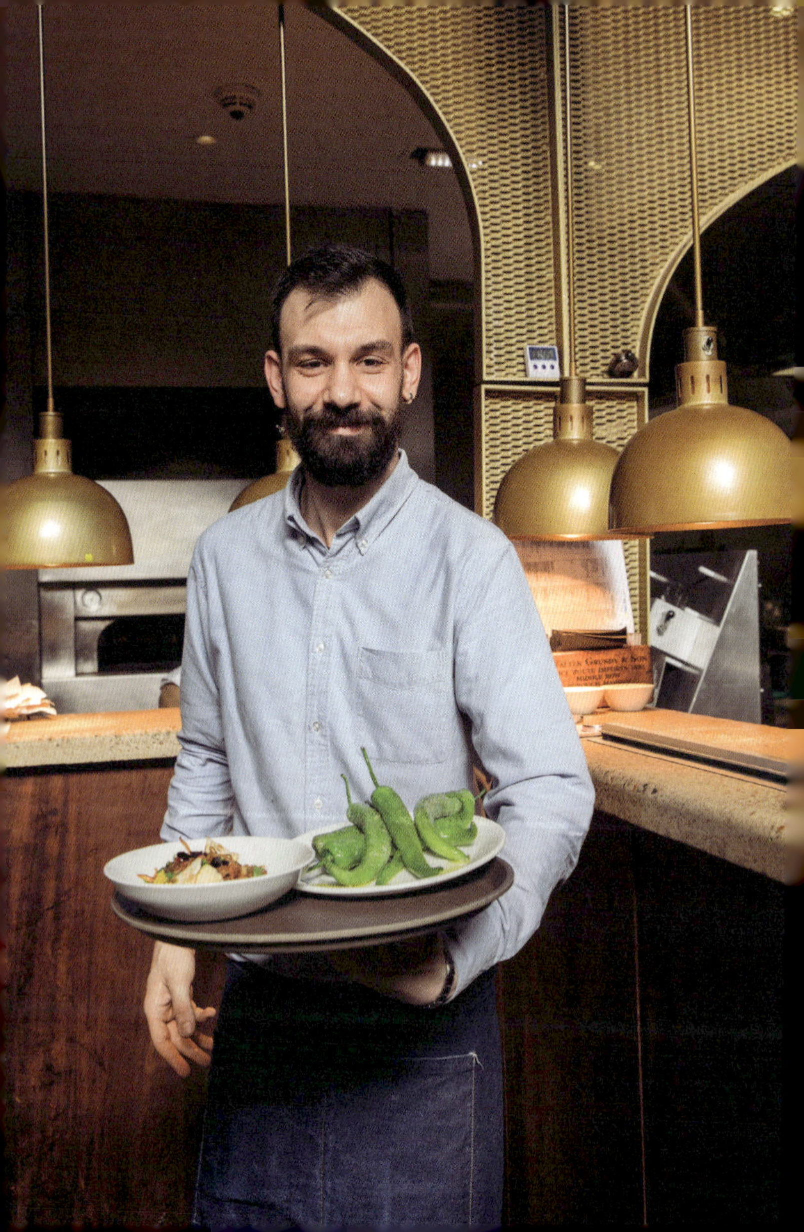

VEGETARIAN AND VEGAN LONDON

Club Mexicana

Inspired by the taquerias of Los Angeles and Mexico City, Club Mexicana is the best place for a good time and vegan Mexican food. The menu is full of favourites such as the beer-battered Tofish or the Cheezeburger Taco, bowls, burritos, and nachos. Mexican beers, frozen Margaritas, and grapefruit Palomas are always on tap. There are three locations to choose from, the one in Spitalfields being the largest.

46-48 Commercial Street, London E1, clubmexicana.com

Plants by DE

Ella Mills, better known as Deliciously Ella, has several plant-based cookery books to her name, as well as a range of healthy snacks that can be found in many supermarkets. This is her first plant-based restaurant. Breakfast, lunch, or dinner, you are in for a vegan treat!

18 Weighhouse St, London W1, deliciouslyella.com

Farmacy

Firmly grounded in Notting Hill, this plant-based restaurant is an absolute treasure trove for vegans. They use ingredients from their own biodynamic farm or from sustainable and economically conscious suppliers. Open for brunch and dinner, serving a range of Farmacy classics from earth bowls to burgers and tacos. For a celebration, you can feast on a vegan afternoon tea.

74-76 Westbourne Grove, London W2, farmacylondon.com

The Gallery Café

With windows overlooking a beautiful English garden, this is a good start to your day. The vegan menu offers breakfast options, and serve good coffee, juices, burgers, sandwiches, pancakes, and pizza. The Cafe is part of St. Margaret's House, a charity that regularly hosts events.

21 Old Ford Rd, London E2, stmargaretshouse.org.uk

Third Culture Deli

The duo behind the vegan cheese brand I Am Nut OK have opened the vegan Third Culture Deli on Broadway Market. And this market should be on your list anyway. They serve coffee, salads, sandwiches, and pastries in a vintage inspired interior. There is limited seating but take-away is always an option.

29 Broadway Market, London E8, thirdculturedeli.com

Facing Heaven

If you like it spicy, go to this vegan Chinese in Hackney. It is named after the Sichuanese 'facing heaven' pepper. They fuse influences from Cantonese, Yunnan, and Shaanxi cuisines, using typical vegan ingredients like mushrooms, cauliflower, and tofu. Absolutely everything on their menu is delicious.

1a Bayford St, London E8, facing-heaven.com

Mallow

When at Borough Market and looking for an amazing vegan restaurant, Mallow is your best bet. It is run by the team behind Mildreds so you can rest assured you are in very capable hands. They offer a varied, plant-based, all-day menu that takes inspiration from all over the world. Shiitake miso croquettes, sweetcorn ribs, pumpkin blossom, beetroot burgers: it will be hard to make a choice. There is also a branch in Canary Wharf.

1 Cathedral St, London SE1, mallowlondon.com

Ravi Shankar Bhelpoori House

Brick Lane is famous for its Bangladeshi and Indian restaurants, but the locals go to Drummond Street for authentic South Asian food. Vegetarians should head to Ravi Shankar Bhelpoori

House. They have been serving vegetarian dishes since the 1980s. It is getting a bit run down, but the weekend buffets are still very in demand and worth the hype.

133-135 Drummond St, London NW1, ravishankarbhelpoori.com

Purezza

When in the mood for pizza, this buzzing place in Camden is definitely the one to go to. On the vegan menu, you can also find salads, pasta, and desserts. Not just the pizzas are incredible, the mac & cheese comes highly recommended too. As does the tiramisu.

45-47 Parkway, London NW1, purezza.co.uk

Manna

This vegan golden oldie can be found hidden in a side street in beautiful Primrose Hill. At nearly fifty years, this must be one of the oldest vegetarian restaurants in the UK. The vegan menu is full of tasty options, but the Sunday Roast is an absolute winner.

4 Erskine Rd, London NW3, mannalondon.co.uk

La Fauxmagerie

If you are vegan and craving cheese: look no further! Not a restaurant, but a vegan cheese shop in ever-popular Cheshire Street. They sell their own brand, as well as many others.

20 Cheshire Street, London E2, lafauxmagerie.com

The Third Estate

A vegan footwear and ethical clothing shop for both men and women. Fashion with a conscience, made from materials like bamboo, hemp, and organic cotton. The brand also sets rigorous ethical standards for their suppliers.

27 Brecknock Rd, London N7, thethirdestate.co.uk

VEGETARIAN AND VEGAN LONDON

OUTSIDE OF LONDON

Bath

Probably Britain's most beautiful city. Bath was founded by the Romans, who used the area's thermal springs to create a spa retreat. It is also known for its outstanding Georgian architecture, with grand squares and imposing crescents. Visit the Roman Baths and the Abbey, and wander through the streets while admiring the architecture. There are direct trains from London Paddington and the journey takes 1 hour and 30 minutes.

Brighton

This was once the seaside escape for the rich and famous, hence the rows of Regency houses, the long-standing Pier, and the grand Royal Pavilion. The pebble beach is perfect for breathing in some fresh air and soaking up the sun. There's some very cool shopping to be done in the independent boutiques, including a lot of vintage and second-hand. The unofficial LBGTQIA+ capital of Britain also has a thriving dining and arts scene, so you will be spoilt for choice. Trains depart from St. Pancras International (stopping at Farringdon, Blackfriars, and London Bridge) and London Victoria. Journey time is an hour.

Cambridge

Cambridge is home to the iconic University of Cambridge. Charles Darwin, Isaac Newton, Robert Oppenheimer, and Stephen Hawking all are Cambridge alumni. In fact, this is where Stephen Hawking spent much of his career studying black holes and cosmology. You should definitely visit some of the colleges. King's College Chapel is an architectural masterpiece. The Mathematical Bridge is a fine example of mathematical and engineering precision. The Fitzwilliam Museum and the Botanical Gardens, with more than 8,000 plant species, are worth a visit too, or you can go punting along the river Cam. Trains depart from King's Cross (50 minutes journey time) and Liverpool Street Station (an hour and 20 minutes).

Hampton Court

hrp.org.uk/ hampton-court-palace

Just outside central London, in Richmond-Upon-Thames, this Grade I-listed palace feels worlds away from the hustle and bustle of the city. Home to British royalty for nearly 500 years, this was Henry VIII's favourite palace. All six of Henry's wives lived here at some point or another. There are beautiful gardens, a famous maze, and perfectly preserved Tudor Kitchens. Imagine the 200 cooks, sergeants, grooms, and pages that worked here to produce over 800 meals a day to feed the household of Henry VIII. Book your tickets in advance. Trains depart from Waterloo Station, with a 30-minute journey time.

Oxford

This picture-perfect university town, larger and busier than Cambridge, is steeped in history, privilege, and prestige. Oxford University is the oldest university in the English-speaking world. Albert Einstein, Oscar Wilde, J.R.R. Tolkien, Anna Wintour, and Hugh Grant all studied here. A tour of the university colleges is a must. Harry Potter fans will certainly recognise several locations used in the films. In Christ Church College you can venture inside the Dining Hall, which is thought to have inspired the movie version of Hogwarts' Great Hall. You can also see the staircase that Harry stood on while speaking to Professor McGonagall in the first film. Do a bit of shopping, and have something to eat in the covered market area, or go punting along the river Isis. You can also visit Blenheim Palace. It is only a short bus ride away and the birthplace of Winston Churchill. Trains depart from London Marylebone and London Paddington with a journey time of an hour.

↓ WHITSTABLE

↓ WHITSTABLE

Whitstable

An incredibly charming seaside town. Pebble beaches, colourful beach huts, fishermen's cottages, a working harbour, and a beachfront promenade provide for the perfect backdrop to take some very pretty pictures. Seafood-lovers will be in in heaven. There really is no better place to tuck into a pint of fresh prawns or feast on half-a-dozen oysters. The Lobster Shack is a bit harder to find, but well worth the effort, especially if you manage to get a seat on the jetty during sunset. There are lots of independent shops and galleries, that is if you manage to drag yourself away from the beachfront. Trains from St. Pancras International, London Bridge, and London Victoria take you to Whitstable in 1 hour 30 minutes.

INDEX

Boroughs 8
Travel 14
Where to stay 18
Good to know 23
When to travel 28
History 40
Sightseeing 48
Museums 54
Street art 62
Cinema 66
Festivals 68
Tours 70
Things to do 72
Famous people 76
Films and series in & about London 82
Books in & about London 86
Fun facts 90
Photo spots 94
Food and Drinks 100
Going out 124
Shopping 134
Green London 166
Parks & swimming 168
Vegetarian and vegan London 176
Outside of London 184

FOOD & DRINKS 100
Afternoon Tea 104-105
Arcade Food Hall 113
Arment, W.J. 107
Banglatown 118-121
BAO 110
Beigel Bake 121
Beppe's Café 103
Bone Daddies 110
Borough Market 115
Breakfast 102-104
Bring the parents 121
Broadway Market 115
Bubblewrap 117
Bun House 116
Buns from Home 105

Cat & Mutton 112
Chinatown 116-118
City Spice 118
Din Tai Fung 109
Dishoom 108
EL & N 105
Fish & Chips 107-108
Flat Iron Square 115
Food Courts & Food Markets 113-115
Garrison, The 112
Gloria 108
Golden Hind 108
Hicce Heart 112
Hung's 118
Kelly, G. 105
Kerb Seven Dials Market 113
Kiln 110
Kitchens at Old Spitalfields Market, The 113
Lahore Kebab House 118
Lunch & Dinner 108-111
Maltby Street Market 115
Mamason's Dirty Ice Cream 116
Manze, M. 107
Mare Street Market 104
OKKO 109
On the Bab 108
Ottolenghi 105
Padella 109
Pellici, E. 103
Pie & Mash 105-107
Plum Valley 116
Poppies 107
Regency Café 103
Sessions Arts Club 121
Sketch 121
Spa Terminus 115
Sunday Roast 112
Sutton & Sons 108
Terry's 103
Trejos Tacos 110

GOING OUT 124
Cadogan Arms, Chelsea, The 129
Churchill Arms, The 129
Clubs 130-133
Corsica Studios 133
Egg London 132
Electric Brixton 133
Fabric 130
Harrison Pub, The 126
Heaven 130
Holly Bush 130
KOKO 132
Ministry of Sound 133
People's Park Tavern, The 127
Pride of Spitalfields 127
Prince of Wales, The 133
Prospect of Whitby 127
Pubs 126-130
Queen of Hoxton 132
Roxy, The 130
Royal Inn on the Park 127
Royal Oak, The 129
Trafalgar Tavern 129
Village Underground 132
XOYO 132

MUSEUMS 54
British Museum 54
Design Museum, The 61
Museum of the Home, The 55
National Gallery 54
National History Museum 60
National Maritime Museum 58
Old Royal Naval College 59
Photographers Gallery, The 61
Queen's House 59
Royal Observatory, The 59
Saatchi Gallery 59
Science Museum 61
Shakespeare's Globe 56
Shard, The 57
Tate Britain 56
Tate Modern 56
Tower Bridge 56
Victoria and Albert Museum 61

White Cube Bermondsey 58
Whitechapel Gallery 54

PHOTO SPOTS 94
Beatles 98
Big Ben 94
Columbia Road Flower Market 98
Harry Potter 98
Leadenhall Market 97
Notting Hill 94
Shoreditch 97
Skyline 98
St. Dunstan-in-the-East 97
St. Paul's Cathedral 94
Tower Bridge 94

SHOPPING 134
How to dress like a local 136

Affordable art & home deco 160
Backyard Market 160
Columbia Road 160
Print Club London 160
Royal Academy of Arts Summer Exhibition 160

ART SUPPLIES 158
Atlantis 159
Choosing Keeping 159
London Graphic Centre 159
McCulloch & Wallis 159
Present & Correct 159

BOOKSHOPS 154
Archive Bookstore 156
Arthur Probstain 155
Booksellers Row, Cecil Court 154
Daunt Books 155
Donlon Books 156
Foyles 154
Gosh! 155
Hatchard's 156
Libreria 156
Stanfords 154
Word on the water 155

DEPARTMENT STORES 152
Fortnum & Mason 153
Hamleys 153
Harrods 153
Liberty 153
Selfridges 153

RECORD SHOPS 162
Reckless Records 163
Rough Trade East 163
Sounds that Swing 163
Third Man Records 163
World of Echo 163

SHOPS WE LOVE 164
House of MinaLima 165
Gods Own Junkyard 165
Lock & Co Hatters 165

STREETWEAR 148
Aries 149
Dover Street Market 149
Footpatrol 149
END 149

VEGETARIAN AND VEGAN LONDON 176
Bubula 177
Club Mexicana 180
Facing Heaven 181
Farmacy 180
Fauxmagerie, La 182
Gallery Café, The 180
Jam Delish 177
Mallow 181
Manna 182
Mildreds 176
Plants by DE 180
Purezza 182
Ravi Shankar Bhelpoori House 181
Sagar 177
Third Culture Deli 181
Third Estate, The 182
Tofu Vegan 177

VINTAGE, SECOND-HAND SHOPS & FLEA MARKETS 138-141
Battersea Boot 143
Beyond Retro 140
Brick Lane Vintage Market 142
Buck Street Market 144
Camden Market 144
Camden Passage 141
Capital Carboot Sale Pimlico 143
Chillie London 141
Clerkenwell Vintage Fashion Fair 141
Dukes Cupboard 140
Hackney Flea Market 142
Nordic Poetry 140
Old Spitalfields 142
Portobello Road Market 143
Rellik 141
Rokit 138
Vinegar Yard 143
Vintage Hackney Wick 140

SIGHTSEEING 48
10 Downing Street 50
British Library, The 51
Buckingham Palace 49
Houses of Parliament 50
St. Paul's Cathedral 48
Tower of London 48
Trafalgar Square 48
Westminster Abbey 49

WHERE TO STAY 18
Astor 19
Buxton, The 20
Culpeper, The 20
Generator Hostel 19
Kip 21
Komo Pod Hotel 21
Mama Shelter 20
Mornington, The 19
New Road Hotel 20
Onefam 19
University halls 20
Wombats the City Hostel 19
Yotel London Shoreditch 20

ABOUT THE AUTHOR

Maaike van Steekelenburg

Maaike van Steekelenburg is a travel journalist who lived in London for many years. She wrote several guidebooks about The Big Smoke before. *Why Should I Go to London* was a precious family project as she compiled this guidebook with her three children, who were born and partially raised in London. Now young adults and students themselves, they return to their hometown whenever they can. Together they have gathered all their favourite spots, allowing you to experience London like a true local.

WHY SHOULD I GO TO LONDON
the city you definitely need to
visit before you turn 30

Published in 2024 by mo'media
P.O. Box 359, 3000 AJ Rotterdam,
The Netherlands, momedia.nl

Concept
mo'media

Text and address selection
Maaike van Steekelenburg

Art direction and illustration design
Jelle F. Post

Editing
Ezra van Wilgenburg

Photography
David in den Bosch, Vincent van den Hoogen, Petra de Hamer, mo'media BV, and others

Special thanks to
Liselot, Joris and Annebel;
Eva van den Berg

All rights reserved. No part of this publication may be copied, displayed, extracted, reproduced, utilised, stored in a retrieval system or transmitted in any form or by any means, electronic, mechanical or otherwise including but not limited to photocopying, recording, or scanning without the prior written permission of the publisher.

Copyright © mo'media BV, 2024

Why Should I Go To London
ISBN 978 94 93 338 098
NUR 510

Disclaimer
The points of interested mentioned in this travel guide have been selected by the authors. None of them have been paid for inclusion in this book: the *Why Should I Go To* book series is entirely ad-free.

Publisher's Note
Every effort has been made to ensure that the information in this book is accurate at the time of going to press. The publisher welcomes any information or suggestions for correction or improvement. Please send us an e-mail at info@momedia.nl or a DM on Instagram.

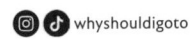

whyshouldigoto